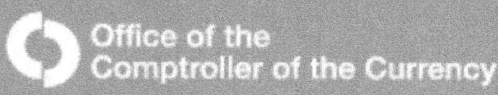

Office of the
Comptroller of the Currency

I0448661

OCC Mortgage Metrics Report

Disclosure of National Bank and Federal Savings
Association Mortgage Loan Data

First Quarter 2014

Office of the Comptroller of the Currency
Washington, D.C.

June 2014

Contents

Executive Summary

This *OCC Mortgage Metrics Report* for the first quarter of 2014 provides performance data on first-lien residential mortgages serviced by selected national banks and one federal savings association. The mortgages in this portfolio comprise 48 percent of all first-lien residential mortgages outstanding in the United States—24.5 million loans totaling $4.1 trillion in unpaid principal. This report presents information on their performance through March 31, 2014.

The performance of mortgages in this portfolio improved for the sixth consecutive quarter. At the end of the first quarter of 2014, 93.1 percent of mortgages serviced by the reporting servicers were current and performing, compared with 91.8 percent at the end of the previous quarter and 90.2 percent a year earlier. The percentage of mortgages that were 30 to 59 days past due decreased 20.9 percent from the previous quarter to 2.1 percent of the portfolio, a 19.8 percent decrease from a year earlier and the lowest since the OCC began reporting mortgage performance data in the first quarter of 2008. The percentage of mortgages included in this report that were seriously delinquent—60 or more days past due or held by bankrupt borrowers whose payments were 30 or more days past due—decreased to 3.1 percent of the portfolio compared with 3.5 percent at the end of the previous quarter and 4.0 percent a year earlier. The percentage of mortgages that were seriously delinquent has decreased 22.4 percent from a year earlier and is at its lowest level since the end of June 2008.

At the end of the first quarter of 2014, the number of mortgages in the process of foreclosure fell to 432,832, a decrease of 52.3 percent from a year earlier. The percentage of mortgages that were in the process of foreclosure at the end of the first quarter of 2014 was 1.8 percent, the lowest level since September 2008. During the quarter, servicers initiated 90,852 new foreclosures—a decrease of 49.1 percent from a year earlier. Factors contributing to the decline include improved economic conditions, aggressive foreclosure prevention assistance, and the transfer of loans to servicers outside the reporting banks and thrift. The number of completed foreclosures decreased to 56,185, a decrease of 7.5 percent from the previous quarter and 33.9 percent from a year earlier.

Servicers implemented 237,133 home retention actions—including modifications, trial-period plans, and shorter-term payment plans—compared with 71,678 home forfeiture actions during the quarter, which include completed foreclosures, short sales, and deed-in-lieu-of-foreclosure actions. The number of home retention actions implemented by servicers decreased by 2.3 percent from the previous quarter and 32.1 percent from a year earlier. Almost 91 percent of modifications in the first quarter of 2014 reduced monthly principal and interest payments; 58.6 percent of modifications reduced payments by 20 percent or more. Modifications reduced payments by $292 per month on average, while modifications made under the Home Affordable Modification Program (HAMP) reduced monthly payments by an average of $312.

Mortgage Performance

- The overall percentage of mortgages in this report that were current and performing increased to 93.1 percent at the end of the first quarter of 2014 (see table 7).

- The percentage of mortgages that were seriously delinquent at the end of the quarter was 3.1 percent, a decrease of 22.4 percent from a year earlier (see table 7).

- The percentage of government-guaranteed mortgages that were current and performing increased to 88.4 percent from 86.2 percent a year earlier (see table 9). Government-guaranteed mortgages compose 24.8 percent of the total serviced portfolio. The percentage of government-guaranteed mortgages that were seriously delinquent decreased 8.5 percent from a year earlier to 5.7 percent of the government-guaranteed mortgages in the portfolio (see table 9).

- Mortgages serviced for Fannie Mae and Freddie Mac (government-sponsored enterprises or GSE) made up 58.9 percent of the mortgages in this report. The percentage of these mortgages that were current and performing was 96.7 percent at the end of the first quarter of 2014, an increase from the previous quarter and from a year earlier (see table 10).

Home Retention Actions: Loan Modifications, Trial-Period Plans, and Payment Plans

- Servicers implemented 237,133 home retention actions—modifications, trial-period plans, and payment plans—during the first quarter of 2014 (see table 1). The number of home retention actions was more than three times the number of completed foreclosures, short sales, and deed-in-lieu-of-foreclosure actions in the quarter (see table 5).

- New home retention actions included 65,437 modifications, 71,381 trial-period plans, and 100,315 payment plans (see table 1). HAMP modifications increased 49.0 percent from the previous quarter to 31,030. Other modifications decreased to 34,407—a decrease of 33.4 percent from the previous quarter and 68.9 percent from a year earlier. HAMP trial-period plans decreased 26.9 percent from the previous quarter to 23,060, up 27.1 percent from the previous year.

Table 1. Number of New Home Retention Actions							
	3/31/13	6/30/13	9/30/13	12/31/13	3/31/14	1Q %Change	1Y %Change
Other Modifications	110,519	85,582	76,134	51,637	34,407	-33.4%	-68.9%
HAMP Modifications	28,030	22,613	23,159	20,829	31,030	49.0%	10.7%
Other Trial-Period Plans	85,516	68,465	62,163	50,743	48,321	-4.8%	-43.5%
HAMP Trial-Period Plans	18,145	32,028	38,804	31,527	23,060	-26.9%	27.1%
Payment Plans	107,113	107,403	112,568	88,093	100,315	13.9%	-6.3%
Total	349,323	316,091	312,828	242,829	237,133	-2.3%	-32.1%

- Servicers reduced interest rates in 73.3 percent of all modifications made during the first quarter of 2014. Servicers used term extensions in 78.0 percent of modifications, principal deferrals in 25.1 percent, and principal reductions in 8.1 percent (see table 17). Among HAMP modifications, servicers reduced interest rates in 85.9 percent of those modifications, deferred principal in 30.1 percent, and reduced principal in 6.8 percent (see table 18).

- Servicers have reduced monthly principal and interest payments in 90.8 percent of modifications made in the quarter (see table 22). Servicers reduced monthly payments by an average of 23.8 percent for all borrowers who qualified for modifications. HAMP modifications reduced payments by an average of 27.1 percent (see table 24).

Modified Loan Performance

- Servicers implemented 3,460,476 modifications from January 1, 2008, through December 31, 2013. Of these modifications, almost 60 percent were active at the end of the first quarter of 2014 and slightly more than 40 percent had exited the portfolios of the reporting institutions, through payment in full, involuntary liquidation—foreclosure, short sale, or deed-in-lieu of foreclosure—or transfer to a non-reporting servicer (see table 2).

- Of the 2,071,078 modifications that were active at the end of the first quarter of 2014, 69.9 percent were current and performing at end of the quarter, 23.9 percent were delinquent, and 6.1 percent were in the process of foreclosure.

- Of the 40 percent of modifications that had exited the portfolio prior to the end of the first quarter of 2014, 8.2 percent had been liquidated involuntarily—through foreclosure, short sale, or deed-in-lieu. Another 3.3 percent had been paid in full and 28.7 percent had been transferred.

Table 2. Status of Mortgages Modified in 2008–4Q 2013									
	Completed Modifications		As Percent of Modifications Active as of 3/31/14				As Percent of All Modifications Completed		
Year	Total	Active at 3/31/14	Current	30–59 Days Delinquent	Seriously Delinquent	Foreclosures in Process	Completed Foreclosures IL*	Paid Off	No Longer in the Portfolio
2008	443,294	147,566	59.5%	9.4%	21.1%	10.0%	17.3%	4.9%	44.5%
2009	593,884	276,567	63.0%	8.6%	19.6%	8.7%	13.6%	4.8%	35.1%
2010	955,422	536,606	68.7%	8.0%	16.4%	6.9%	9.2%	3.8%	30.9%
2011	569,553	371,910	70.1%	7.7%	15.8%	6.4%	4.9%	3.0%	26.7%
2012	479,820	374,635	73.8%	7.5%	13.9%	4.8%	1.6%	1.9%	18.5%
2013	418,503	363,794	77.0%	8.5%	11.8%	2.7%	0.3%	0.8%	12.0%
Total	3,460,476	2,071,078	69.9%	8.1%	15.8%	6.1%	8.2%	3.3%	28.7%
HAMP Modification Performance Compared With Other Modifications*									
HAMP	781,872	502,478	80.9%	6.3%	9.0%	3.8%	3.7%	2.0%	30.1%
Other**	1,897,464	1,280,979	67.8%	8.6%	17.4%	6.3%	6.9%	3.3%	22.3%
Modifications That Reduced Payments by 10 Percent or More									
	2,222,103	1,413,535	74.7%	7.6%	12.8%	4.9%	5.6%	2.5%	28.3%
Modifications That Reduced Payments by Less Than 10 Percent									
	1,238,373	657,543	59.7%	9.2%	22.2%	8.9%	12.8%	4.9%	29.3%

*Completed foreclosures or other involuntarily liquidated mortgages.

**Modifications used to compare with HAMP modifications include only modifications implemented from the third quarter of 2009 through the fourth quarter of 2013.

- HAMP modifications implemented since the third quarter of 2009 have performed better than other modifications (see table 2). HAMP modifications perform better because of the emphasis on reduced monthly payments, affordability relative to income, income verification, and successful completion of a trial period. While HAMP modifications generally reduce the borrowers' monthly payments more and perform better over time, more restrictive criteria limit the number of borrowers who may qualify for a HAMP modification.

- Modifications that reduced borrowers' monthly payments by 10 percent or more performed significantly better than other modifications that reduced monthly payments by less than 10 percent. Of the 1,413,535 modifications that reduced payments by 10 percent or more and were active at the end of the first quarter of 2014, 74.7 percent were current, compared with 59.7 percent of modifications that reduced payments by less than 10 percent (see table 2).

- Modifications on mortgages owned by the servicers and those serviced for the GSEs performed better than other modifications. Of the modifications implemented from January 1, 2008, 19.7 percent of modifications on mortgages held in the servicers' own portfolios, 23.4 percent of Fannie Mae mortgages, and 22.3 percent of Freddie Mac mortgages were 60 or more days delinquent after 12 months. Conversely, 43.3 percent of government-guaranteed mortgages and 38.4 percent of private investor-held loans were 60 or more days delinquent after 12 months. This variance reflects differences in the loans and borrowers, the modification programs, and the servicers' flexibility to modify loans they own (see table 3).

Table 3. Re-Default Rates for Portfolio Loans and Loans Serviced for Others (60 or More Days Delinquent)*					
Investor Loan Type	6 Months After Modification	12 Months After Modification	18 Months After Modification	24 Months After Modification	36 Months After Modification
Fannie Mae	16.3%	23.4%	26.7%	27.5%	27.4%
Freddie Mac	15.6%	22.3%	25.9%	27.3%	27.6%
Government-Guaranteed	29.4%	43.3%	49.6%	51.7%	53.0%
Private	28.9%	38.4%	43.8%	45.5%	48.2%
Portfolio Loans	12.7%	19.7%	24.1%	26.2%	26.8%
Overall	21.8%	30.8%	35.6%	37.3%	38.6%

*Data include all modifications made since January 1, 2008 that have aged the indicated number of months.

Foreclosures and Other Home Forfeiture Actions

- Newly initiated foreclosures decreased 27.0 percent from the previous quarter and 49.1 percent from a year earlier. The number of foreclosures in process decreased 17.3 percent from the previous quarter and 52.3 percent from a year earlier (see table 4). Factors contributing to the decline include improved economic conditions, foreclosure prevention assistance, and transfer of loans outside the reporting institutions.

Table 4. New Foreclosures and Foreclosures in Process							
	3/31/13	6/30/13	9/30/13	12/31/13	3/31/14	1Q %Change	1Y %Change
Newly Initiated Foreclosures	178,360	150,592	130,592	124,468	90,852	-27.0%	-49.1%
Foreclosures in Process	907,228	744,369	604,763	523,528	432,832	-17.3%	-52.3%

- Home forfeiture actions totaled 71,678 at the end of the quarter, a decrease of 14.7 percent from the previous quarter and 45.6 percent from a year earlier. Completed foreclosures decreased 7.5 percent from the previous quarter and 33.9 percent from a year earlier. Short sales decreased 68.4 percent from a year earlier. Short sales composed 19.0 percent of home forfeiture actions completed in the first quarter of 2014 (see table 5).

Table 5. Completed Foreclosures and Other Home Forfeiture Actions							
	3/31/13	6/30/13	9/30/13	12/31/13	3/31/14	1Q %Change	1Y %Change
Completed Foreclosures	84,977	79,960	82,841	60,765	56,185	-7.5%	-33.9%
New Short Sales	43,143	39,207	31,261	21,149	13,613	-35.6%	-68.4%
New Deed-in-Lieu-of-Foreclosure Actions	3,596	2,579	2,112	2,117	1,880	-11.2%	-47.7%
Total	131,716	121,746	116,214	84,031	71,678	-14.7%	-45.6%

About Mortgage Metrics

The *OCC Mortgage Metrics Report* presents data on first-lien residential mortgages serviced by seven national banks and a federal savings association with the largest mortgage-servicing portfolios.[1] The data represent 48 percent of all first-lien residential mortgages outstanding in the country and focus on credit performance, loss mitigation efforts, and foreclosures. Ninety-one percent of the mortgages in the portfolio were serviced for investors other than the reporting institutions. At the end of the first quarter of 2014, the reporting institutions serviced 24.5 million first-lien mortgage loans, totaling $4.1 trillion in unpaid principal (see table 6).

The loans reflected in this report represent a large percentage of the overall mortgage industry, but they do not represent a statistically random sample of all mortgage loans. The characteristics of these loans may differ from the overall population of mortgages. This report does not attempt to quantify or adjust for known seasonal effects that occur within the mortgage industry.

In addition to providing information to the public, the report and its data support the supervision of national bank and federal savings association mortgage-servicing practices. Examiners use the data to help assess emerging trends, identify anomalies, compare servicers with peers, evaluate asset quality and necessary loan-loss reserves, and assess loss mitigation actions.

The report promotes the use of standardized terms and elements, which allow better comparisons across the industry and over time. The report uses standardized definitions for prime, Alt-A, and subprime mortgages based on commonly used credit score ranges.

The Office of the Comptroller of the Currency (OCC) and the participating institutions devote significant resources to ensuring that the information is reliable and accurate. Steps to ensure the validity of the data include quality assurance processes conducted by the banks and savings association, comprehensive data validation tests performed by a third-party data aggregator, and comparisons with the institutions' quarterly call reports. Data sets of this size and scope inevitably incur some degree of imperfections. The OCC requires servicers to adjust previous data submissions when errors and omissions are detected. In some cases, data presented in this report reflect resubmissions from institutions that restate and correct earlier information.

The report also includes mortgage modification data by state and territories in appendix E. These data fulfill reporting requirements in the Dodd–Frank Wall Street Reform and Consumer Protection Act of 2010 (Public Law 111-203).

Definitions and Method

The report uses standard definitions for three categories of mortgage creditworthiness based on the following ranges of borrowers' credit scores at the time of origination:

---

[1] The seven national banks are Bank of America, JPMorgan Chase, Citibank, HSBC, PNC, U.S. Bank, and Wells Fargo. The federal savings association is OneWest Bank.

- **Prime**—660 and above.

- **Alt-A**—620 to 659.

- **Subprime**—below 620.

Approximately 9 percent of mortgages in the portfolio lack credit scores at origination and are classified as "other." This group includes a mix of prime, Alt-A, and subprime mortgages. The lack of credit scores often results from acquisitions of portfolios from third parties for which borrower credit scores at origination were not available.

Additional definitions include:

- **Completed foreclosures**—Ownership of properties transferred to servicers or investors. The ultimate result is the loss of borrowers' homes because of nonpayment.

- **Deed-in-lieu-of-foreclosure actions**—Actions in which borrowers transfer ownership of the properties (deeds) to servicers in full satisfaction of the outstanding mortgage debt to lessen the adverse impact of the debt on borrowers' credit records. Deed-in-lieu-of-foreclosure actions typically have a less adverse impact than foreclosures on borrowers' credit records.

- **Foreclosures in process**—Number of mortgages for which servicers have begun formal foreclosure proceedings but have not yet completed the foreclosure process. The foreclosure process varies by state and can take 15 months or more to complete. Many foreclosures in process never result in the loss of borrowers' homes because servicers simultaneously pursue other loss mitigation actions, and borrowers may return their mortgages to current and performing status.

- **Government-guaranteed mortgages**—All mortgages with an explicit guaranty from the U.S. government, including the Federal Housing Administration (FHA), the Department of Veterans Affairs (VA), and, to a lesser extent, certain other departments. These loans may be held in pools backing Government National Mortgage Association (Ginnie Mae) securities, owned by or securitized through different third-party investors, or held in the portfolios of reporting institutions.

- **Home retention actions**—Loan modifications, trial-period plans, and payment plans that allow borrowers to retain ownership and occupancy of their homes while attempting to return the loans to a current and performing status.

- **Loan modifications**—Actions that contractually change the terms of mortgages with respect to interest rates, maturity, principal, or other terms of the loan.

- **Newly initiated foreclosures**—Mortgages for which the servicers initiate formal foreclosure proceedings during the quarter. Many newly initiated foreclosures do not result in the loss of borrowers' homes because servicers simultaneously pursue other loss mitigation actions, and borrowers may act to return their mortgages to current and performing status.

- **Payment plans**—Short-to-medium-term changes in scheduled terms and payments in order to return mortgages to a current and performing status.

- **Payment-option, adjustable rate mortgages (ARM)**—Mortgages that allow borrowers to choose a monthly payment that may initially reduce principal, pay interest only, or result in negative amortization, when some amount of unpaid interest is added to the unpaid principal of the loan and results in an increased balance.

- **Principal deferral modifications**—Modifications that remove a portion of the unpaid principal from the amount used to calculate monthly principal and interest payments for a set period. The deferred amount becomes due at the end of the loan term.

- **Principal reduction modifications**—Modifications that permanently forgive a portion of the unpaid principal owed on a mortgage.

- **Re-default rates**—Percentage of modified loans that subsequently become delinquent or enter the foreclosure process. As measures of delinquency, this report presents re-default rates using 30, 60, and 90 or more days delinquent and in process of foreclosure. It focuses on the 60-day-delinquent measure. All re-default data presented in this report are based on modified loans in effect for the specified amount of time after the modification. All loans that have been repaid in full, been refinanced, been sold, or completed the foreclosure process are removed from the calculation. Data include only modifications that have had time to age the indicated number of months following the modification.

- **Seriously delinquent loans**—Mortgages that are 60 or more days past due, and all mortgages held by bankrupt borrowers whose payments are 30 or more days past due.

- **Short sales**—Sales of the mortgaged properties at prices that net less than the total amount due on the mortgages. Servicers and borrowers negotiate repayment programs, forbearance, or forgiveness for any remaining deficiency on the debt. Short sales typically have a less adverse impact than foreclosures on borrowers' credit records.

- **Trial-period plans**—Home retention actions that allow borrowers to demonstrate capability and willingness to pay their modified mortgages for a set period of time. The action becomes permanent following the successful completion of the trial period.

Loan delinquencies are reported using the Mortgage Bankers Association convention that a loan is past due when a scheduled payment has not been made by the due date of the following scheduled payment. The statistics and calculated ratios are based on the number of loans rather than on the dollar amount outstanding.

Percentages are rounded to one decimal place unless the result is less than 0.1 percent, which is rounded to two decimal places. The report uses whole numbers when approximating. Values in tables may not total 100 percent because of rounding.

In tables throughout this report, the quarters are indicated by the last day of the quarter (e.g., 3/31/14), quarter-to-quarter changes are shown under the "1Q %Change" column, and year-to-year changes are shown under the "1Y %Change" column.

In tables throughout this report, percentages shown under "1Q %Change" and "1Y %Change" are calculated using actual data, not the rounded values reported for each quarter. Calculating period-to-period changes from the rounded values reported in the tables may yield materially different values than those values indicated in the table.

Mortgage Metrics Report data may not agree with other published data because of timing differences in updating servicer-processing systems.

PART 1: Mortgage Performance

Part I describes the performance of the overall mortgage portfolio, mortgages owned and held by the reporting banks and savings association, government-guaranteed mortgages, mortgages serviced for the GSEs, and mortgages within each risk category.

Overall Mortgage Portfolio

At the end of the first quarter of 2014, the portfolio of mortgages in this report included 24.5 million loans with $4.1 trillion in unpaid principal. The number of mortgages in the portfolio decreased 1.6 percent from the previous quarter and 12.3 percent from a year earlier. The unpaid principal of those loans decreased 1.8 percent from the previous quarter and 12.9 percent from a year earlier. Prime loans were 75 percent of the portfolio at the end of the quarter. Subprime loans were 6 percent of the portfolio, while Alt-A loans were 10 percent. The percentage of prime loans has increased because of higher defaults of lower quality loans, increased origination of prime loans, and some loans being sold to nonreporting servicers.

Table 6. Overall Mortgage Portfolio					
	3/31/13	6/30/13	9/30/13	12/31/13	3/31/14
Total Servicing (Millions)	$4,740,528	$4,507,984	$4,357,767	$4,205,140	$4,129,719
Total Servicing (Number of Loans)	27,941,336	26,528,415	25,643,169	24,902,063	24,503,971
Composition (Percentage of All Mortgages in the Portfolio)					
Prime	73%	73%	74%	75%	75%
Alt-A	11%	10%	10%	10%	10%
Subprime	7%	7%	6%	6%	6%
Other	10%	10%	9%	9%	9%
Composition (Number of Loans in Each Risk Category of the Portfolio)					
Prime	20,284,238	19,451,032	18,973,544	18,598,018	18,387,920
Alt-A	2,993,971	2,781,584	2,631,270	2,529,860	2,482,088
Subprime	1,908,482	1,749,154	1,630,463	1,522,461	1,463,816
Other	2,754,645	2,546,645	2,407,892	2,251,724	2,170,147

Figure 1. Portfolio Composition
Percentage of All Mortgage Loans in the Portfolio

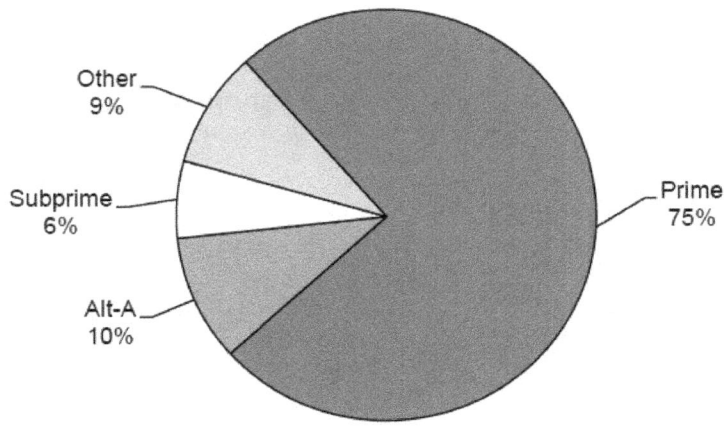

Overall Mortgage Performance

The overall performance of mortgages included in this report has improved for six consecutive quarters. The percentage of mortgages that were current and performing at the end of the quarter was 93.1 percent, compared with 91.8 percent in the previous quarter and 90.2 percent a year earlier. The percentage of mortgages that were 30 to 59 days past due was 2.1 percent, a decrease of 20.9 percent from the previous quarter and 19.8 percent from a year earlier. The percentage of mortgages that were seriously delinquent was 3.1 percent, a decrease of 11.2 percent from the previous quarter and 22.4 percent from a year earlier. The percentage of mortgages in the foreclosure process at the end of the quarter was 1.8 percent, a decrease of 16.0 percent from the previous quarter and 45.6 percent from a year earlier.

Table 7. Overall Portfolio Performance							
(Percentage of Mortgages in the Portfolio)							
	3/31/13	6/30/13	9/30/13	12/31/13	3/31/14	1Q %Change	1Y %Change
Current and Performing	90.2%	90.6%	91.4%	91.8%	93.1%	1.4%	3.2%
30–59 Days Delinquent	2.6%	2.9%	2.6%	2.6%	2.1%	-20.9%	-19.8%
The Following Three Categories Are Classified as Seriously Delinquent							
60–89 Days Delinquent	0.9%	0.9%	0.9%	1.0%	0.7%	-22.8%	-17.3%
90 or More Days Delinquent	2.1%	1.9%	1.8%	1.7%	1.6%	-6.6%	-24.7%
Bankruptcy 30 or More Days Delinquent	1.0%	1.0%	0.9%	0.8%	0.8%	-7.2%	-22.1%
Subtotal for Seriously Delinquent	**4.0%**	**3.8%**	**3.6%**	**3.5%**	**3.1%**	**-11.2%**	**-22.4%**
Foreclosures in Process	3.2%	2.8%	2.4%	2.1%	1.8%	-16.0%	-45.6%
(Number of Mortgages in the Portfolio)							
Current and Performing	25,198,157	24,024,452	23,435,693	22,859,232	22,805,058	-0.2%	-9.5%
30–59 Days Delinquent	717,532	760,078	673,117	648,294	504,718	-22.1%	-29.7%
The Following Three Categories Are Classified as Seriously Delinquent							
60–89 Days Delinquent	248,454	243,832	239,904	237,412	180,269	-24.1%	-27.4%
90 or More Days Delinquent	591,879	499,148	456,887	425,347	391,013	-8.1%	-33.9%
Bankruptcy 30 or More Days Delinquent	278,086	256,536	232,805	208,250	190,081	-8.7%	-31.6%
Subtotal for Seriously Delinquent	**1,118,419**	**999,516**	**929,596**	**871,009**	**761,363**	**-12.6%**	**-31.9%**
Foreclosures in Process	907,228	744,369	604,763	523,528	432,832	-17.3%	-52.3%
Total	27,941,336	26,528,415	25,643,169	24,902,063	24,503,971	-1.6%	-12.3%

Figure 2. Overall Portfolio Performance

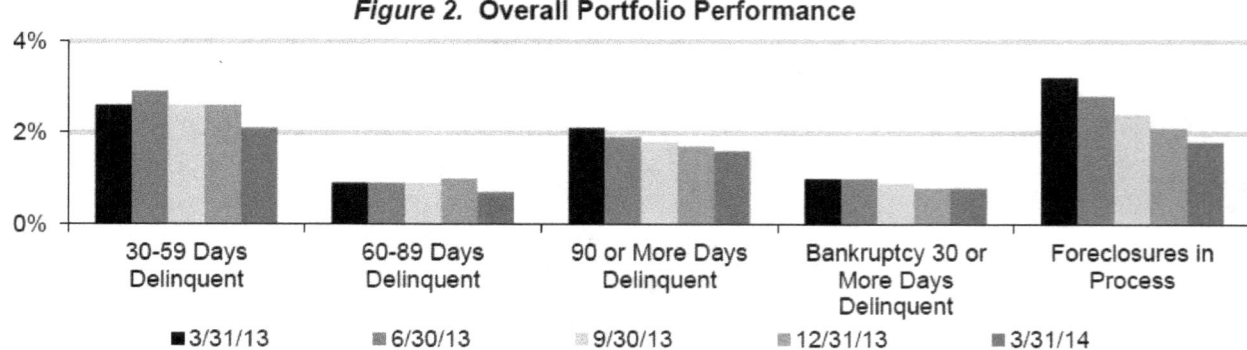

■3/31/13   ■6/30/13   ▨9/30/13   ■12/31/13   ■3/31/14

Performance of Mortgages Held by Reporting Banks and Thrift

The eight reporting institutions owned 9.0 percent of the mortgages in this report at the end of the quarter, an increase in share from 8.8 percent a year earlier. The percentage of these mortgages that were current at the end of the quarter was 88.5 percent. The percentage of these mortgages that were 30 to 59 days delinquent was 2.8 percent, a decrease of 10.6 percent from a year earlier. The percentage of these mortgages that were seriously delinquent was 5.1 percent, a decrease of 6.8 percent from a year earlier. The percentage of these mortgages in the process of foreclosure was 3.6 percent, a decrease of 24.8 percent from a year earlier. Since 2009, mortgages owned by the servicers have performed more poorly than mortgages serviced for GSEs because of concentrations in nontraditional loans, weaker markets, and delinquent loans repurchased from investors.

Table 8. Performance of Mortgages Held by Reporting Banks and Thrift (Percentage)*							
	3/31/13	6/30/13	9/30/13	12/31/13	3/31/14	1Q %Change	1Y %Change
Current and Performing	86.6%	86.6%	87.1%	87.4%	88.5%	1.2%	2.2%
30–59 Days Delinquent	3.1%	3.4%	3.3%	3.3%	2.8%	-13.8%	-10.6%
The Following Three Categories Are Classified as Seriously Delinquent							
60–89 Days Delinquent	1.2%	1.3%	1.3%	1.4%	1.2%	-16.4%	-4.5%
90 or More Days Delinquent	2.7%	2.6%	2.6%	2.5%	2.5%	-0.7%	-9.5%
Bankruptcy 30 or More Days Delinquent	1.5%	1.6%	1.6%	1.5%	1.5%	-2.4%	-3.9%
Subtotal for Seriously Delinquent	5.5%	5.5%	5.5%	5.4%	5.1%	-5.2%	-6.8%
Foreclosures in Process	4.8%	4.5%	4.2%	3.9%	3.6%	-7.9%	-24.8%
Performance of Mortgages Held by Reporting Banks and Thrift (Number)							
Current and Performing	2,133,762	2,059,325	1,997,134	1,943,856	1,949,937	0.3%	-8.6%
30–59 Days Delinquent	77,577	80,314	74,648	72,595	62,004	-14.6%	-20.1%
The Following Three Categories Are Classified as Seriously Delinquent							
60–89 Days Delinquent	30,218	30,784	30,782	31,121	25,801	-17.1%	-14.6%
90 or More Days Delinquent	67,270	62,544	59,376	55,269	54,412	-1.6%	-19.1%
Bankruptcy 30 or More Days Delinquent	37,976	36,970	35,591	33,736	32,635	-3.3%	-14.1%
Subtotal for Seriously Delinquent	135,464	130,298	125,749	120,126	112,848	-6.1%	-16.7%
Foreclosures in Process	118,292	107,493	95,643	87,120	79,569	-8.7%	-32.7%
Total	2,465,095	2,377,430	2,293,174	2,223,697	2,204,358	-0.9%	-10.6%

*The data in this table exclude government-guaranteed mortgages owned and held by the reporting institutions.

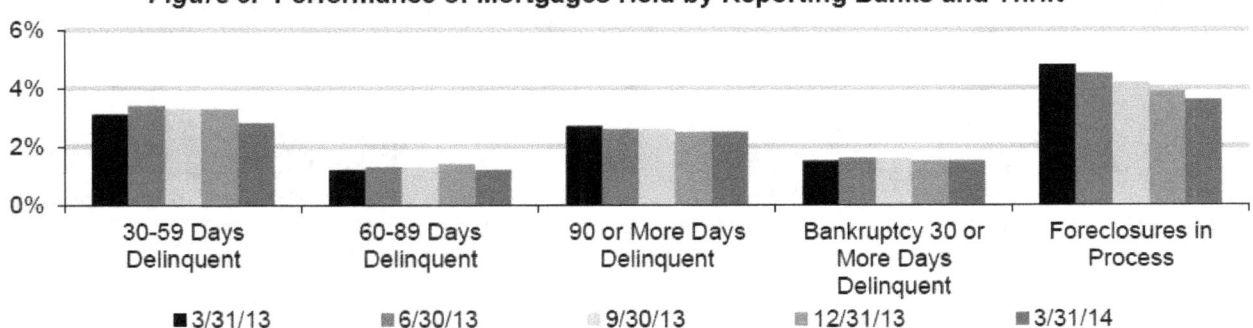

Figure 3. Performance of Mortgages Held by Reporting Banks and Thrift

Performance of Government-Guaranteed Mortgages

Government-guaranteed mortgages were 24.8 percent of the loans in this report at the end of the first quarter of 2014, an increase in share from 24.5 percent a year ago. The percentage of these mortgages that were current at the end of the quarter was 88.4 percent, up from 86.2 percent a year earlier. The percentage of loans that were 30 to 59 days delinquent was 3.5 percent at the end of the quarter, a decrease of 24.0 percent from the previous quarter and 13.5 percent from a year earlier. The percentage of these loans that were seriously delinquent was 5.7 percent, a decrease of 13.4 percent from the previous quarter and 8.5 percent from a year earlier. The percentage of these loans in the process of foreclosure was 2.4 percent, a decrease of 31.1 percent from a year earlier.

Table 9. Performance of Government-Guaranteed Mortgages (Percentage)							
	3/31/13	6/30/13	9/30/13	12/31/13	3/31/14	1Q %Change	1Y %Change
Current and Performing	86.2%	85.7%	86.2%	86.1%	88.4%	2.7%	2.5%
30–59 Days Delinquent	4.1%	4.8%	4.5%	4.6%	3.5%	-24.0%	-13.5%
The Following Three Categories Are Classified as Seriously Delinquent							
60–89 Days Delinquent	1.4%	1.6%	1.7%	1.8%	1.3%	-26.6%	-6.7%
90 or More Days Delinquent	3.6%	3.4%	3.4%	3.6%	3.2%	-10.3%	-11.6%
Bankruptcy 30 or More Days Delinquent	1.2%	1.2%	1.2%	1.2%	1.2%	-3.3%	-1.1%
Subtotal for Seriously Delinquent	6.2%	6.2%	6.3%	6.5%	5.7%	-13.4%	-8.5%
Foreclosures in Process	3.6%	3.3%	2.9%	2.8%	2.4%	-11.8%	-31.1%
Performance of Government-Guaranteed Mortgages (Number)							
Current and Performing	5,897,284	5,592,058	5,398,697	5,274,464	5,371,735	1.8%	-8.9%
30–59 Days Delinquent	277,426	313,250	284,697	282,698	213,169	-24.6%	-23.2%
The Following Three Categories Are Classified as Seriously Delinquent							
60–89 Days Delinquent	95,947	102,475	105,993	109,272	79,494	-27.3%	-17.1%
90 or More Days Delinquent	246,953	222,428	213,035	217,842	193,907	-11.0%	-21.5%
Bankruptcy 30 or More Days Delinquent	80,962	81,430	77,129	74,144	71,104	-4.1%	-12.2%
Subtotal for Seriously Delinquent	423,862	406,333	396,157	401,258	344,505	-14.1%	-18.7%
Foreclosures in Process	243,132	216,324	181,965	170,180	148,859	-12.5%	-38.8%
Total	6,841,704	6,527,965	6,261,516	6,128,600	6,078,268	-0.8%	-11.2%

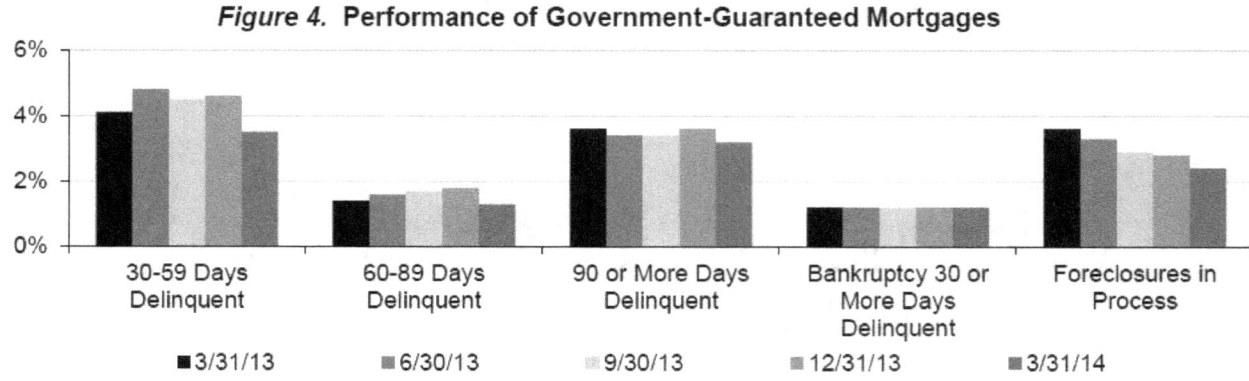

Figure 4. Performance of Government-Guaranteed Mortgages

Performance of GSE Mortgages

GSE mortgages made up 58.9 percent of the mortgages in this report, an increase in share from 56.6 percent a year earlier. GSE mortgages perform better than the overall portfolio because they contain more prime loans. The percentage of GSE mortgages that were current at the end of the quarter was 96.7 percent, up from 94.6 percent a year earlier. The percentage of GSE mortgages that were 30 to 59 days delinquent was 1.1 percent, a decrease of 26.2 percent from a year earlier. The percentage of GSE mortgages that were seriously delinquent was 1.3 percent at the end of the quarter, a decrease of 30.9 percent from a year earlier. The percentage of these loans in the foreclosure process was 0.9 percent, a decrease of 54.2 percent from a year earlier. Fifty-seven percent of the GSE mortgages were serviced for Fannie Mae and 43 percent for Freddie Mac.

Table 10. Performance of GSE Mortgages (Percentage)							
	3/31/13	6/30/13	9/30/13	12/31/13	3/31/14	1Q %Change	1Y %Change
Current and Performing	94.6%	95.1%	95.7%	95.9%	96.7%	0.8%	2.1%
30–59 Days Delinquent	1.5%	1.6%	1.4%	1.4%	1.1%	-21.1%	-26.2%
The Following Three Categories Are Classified as Seriously Delinquent							
60–89 Days Delinquent	0.5%	0.4%	0.4%	0.5%	0.4%	-22.5%	-24.6%
90 or More Days Delinquent	0.9%	0.8%	0.7%	0.6%	0.6%	-1.4%	-31.4%
Bankruptcy 30 or More Days Delinquent	0.5%	0.5%	0.4%	0.4%	0.3%	-14.0%	-35.6%
Subtotal for Seriously Delinquent	**1.9%**	**1.7%**	**1.5%**	**1.5%**	**1.3%**	**-11.2%**	**-30.9%**
Foreclosures in Process	1.9%	1.5%	1.3%	1.2%	0.9%	-24.8%	-54.2%
Performance of GSE Mortgages (Number)							
Current and Performing	14,970,222	14,415,761	14,202,109	14,068,620	13,943,433	-0.9%	-6.9%
30–59 Days Delinquent	244,073	248,747	212,335	211,814	164,306	-22.4%	-32.7%
The Following Three Categories Are Classified as Seriously Delinquent							
60–89 Days Delinquent	74,386	67,829	65,255	67,106	51,148	-23.8%	-31.2%
90 or More Days Delinquent	145,282	113,809	101,216	93,692	90,828	-3.1%	-37.5%
Bankruptcy 30 or More Days Delinquent	83,583	70,996	63,155	57,990	49,057	-15.4%	-41.3%
Subtotal for Seriously Delinquent	**303,251**	**252,634**	**229,626**	**218,788**	**191,033**	**-12.7%**	**-37.0%**
Foreclosures in Process	302,270	233,967	189,610	170,779	126,306	-26.0%	-58.2%
Total	15,819,816	15,151,109	14,833,680	14,670,001	14,425,078	-1.7%	-8.8%

Figure 5. Performance of GSE Mortgages

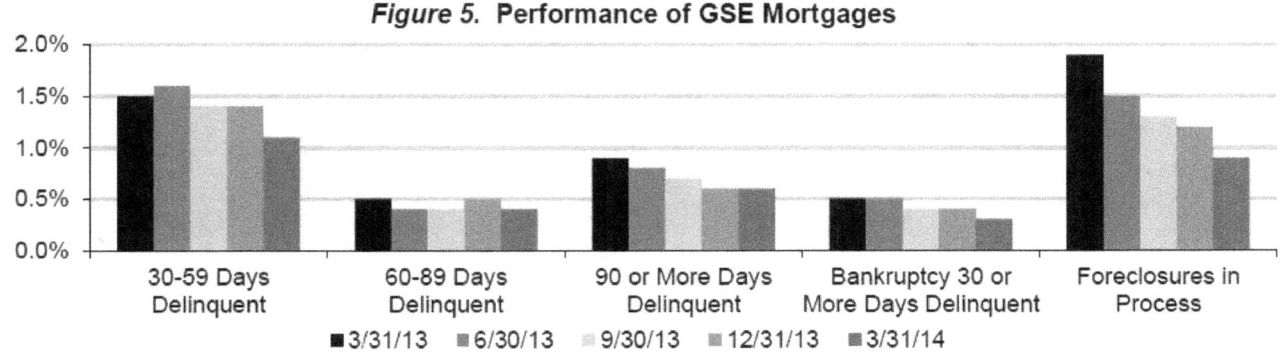

Seriously Delinquent Mortgages, by Risk Category

The portfolio contained 357,056 fewer seriously delinquent loans at the end of the first quarter of 2014 than a year earlier—a 31.9 percent decrease. Seriously delinquent loans were 3.1 percent of the portfolio at the end of the quarter, a decrease of 22.4 percent from a year earlier and the lowest level since the second quarter of 2008. The number of seriously delinquent loans decreased from the previous quarter and the previous year across all risk categories.

Table 11. Seriously Delinquent Mortgages, by Risk Category							
(Percentage of Mortgages in Each Category)							
	3/31/13	6/30/13	9/30/13	12/31/13	3/31/14	1Q %Change	1Y %Change
Prime	2.1%	1.9%	1.8%	1.6%	1.5%	-9.5%	-30.1%
Alt-A	8.4%	8.3%	8.3%	8.4%	7.4%	-11.8%	-12.4%
Subprime	14.6%	14.5%	14.6%	14.7%	13.0%	-11.5%	-10.7%
Other	5.6%	5.6%	5.7%	5.7%	5.2%	-8.6%	-7.5%
Overall	4.0%	3.8%	3.6%	3.5%	3.1%	-11.2%	-22.4%
(Number of Mortgages in Each Category)							
Prime	431,353	372,519	335,590	305,796	273,518	-10.6%	-36.6%
Alt-A	252,990	231,168	218,764	212,203	183,670	-13.4%	-27.4%
Subprime	278,647	254,085	238,446	224,412	190,956	-14.9%	-31.5%
Other	155,429	141,744	136,796	128,598	113,219	-12.0%	-27.2%
Total	1,118,419	999,516	929,596	871,009	761,363	-12.6%	-31.9%

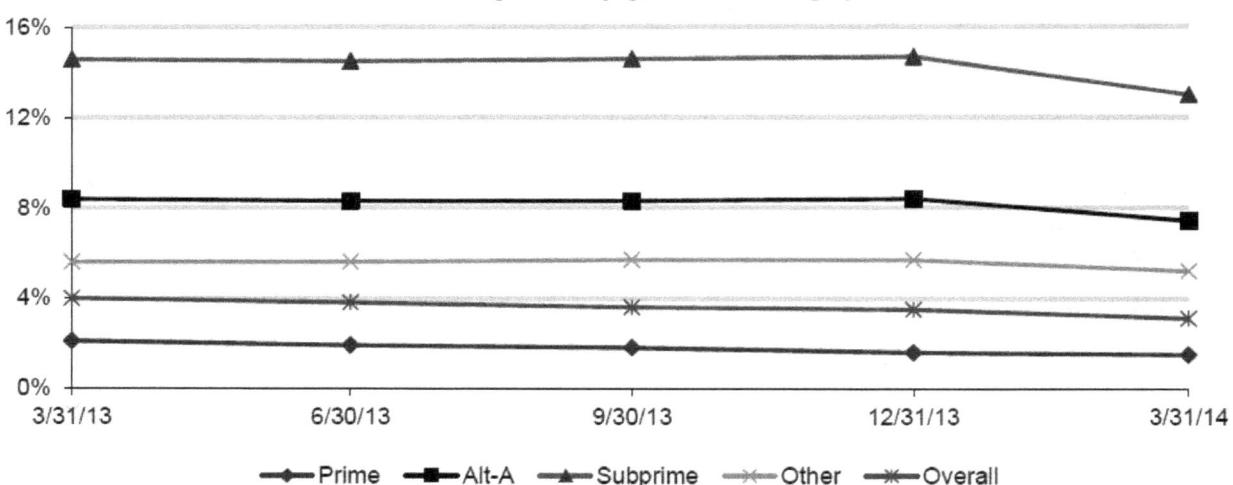

Figure 6. Seriously Delinquent Mortgages, by Risk Category
Percentage of Mortgages in Each Category

Mortgages 30 to 59 Days Delinquent, by Risk Category

The percentage of loans that were 30 to 59 days delinquent was 2.1 percent of the portfolio at the end of the first quarter of 2014, a decrease of 19.8 percent from a year earlier. Early stage delinquencies decreased across all risk categories from the previous quarter and the previous year across all risk categories.

Table 12. Mortgages 30 to 59 Days Delinquent, by Risk Category							
(Percentage of Mortgages in Each Category)							
	3/31/13	6/30/13	9/30/13	12/31/13	3/31/14	1Q %Change	1Y %Change
Prime	1.3%	1.4%	1.3%	1.3%	1.0%	-20.5%	-23.1%
Alt-A	5.7%	6.6%	6.2%	6.4%	5.0%	-21.8%	-12.4%
Subprime	8.6%	10.0%	9.5%	9.6%	7.8%	-18.8%	-9.9%
Other	4.2%	4.8%	4.6%	4.6%	3.7%	-19.4%	-10.8%
Overall	2.6%	2.9%	2.6%	2.6%	2.1%	-20.9%	-19.8%
(Number of Mortgages in Each Category)							
Prime	267,211	279,111	244,277	236,900	186,187	-21.4%	-30.3%
Alt-A	170,084	184,916	164,185	161,013	123,503	-23.3%	-27.4%
Subprime	164,998	174,660	154,832	146,067	114,042	-21.9%	-30.9%
Other	115,239	121,391	109,823	104,314	80,986	-22.4%	-29.7%
Total	717,532	760,078	673,117	648,294	504,718	-22.1%	-29.7%

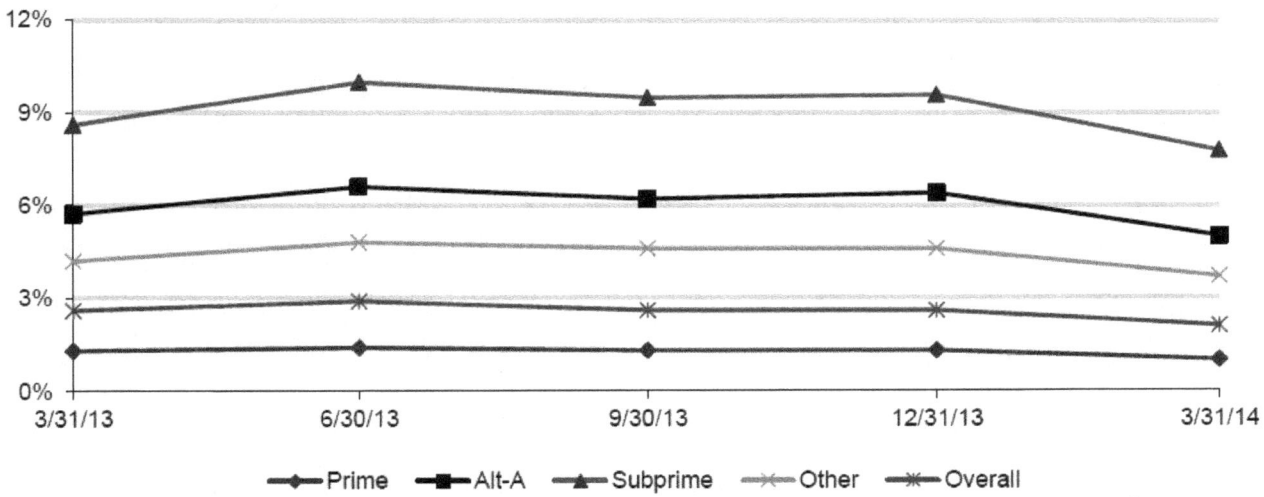

Figure 7. Mortgages 30 to 59 Days Delinquent, by Risk Category
Percentage of Mortgages in Each Category

PART II: Home Retention Actions

Home retention actions include loan modifications, in which servicers modify one or more mortgage contract terms; trial-period plans, in which the loans will be converted to modifications upon successful completion of the trial periods; and payment plans, in which no terms are contractually modified but borrowers are given time to catch up on missed payments. All of these actions can help the borrower become current on the loan, attain payment sustainability, and retain the home.

A. Loan Modifications, Trial-Period Plans, and Payment Plans

New Home Retention Actions

Servicers implemented 237,133 home retention actions—loan modifications, trial-period plans, and payment plans—during the first quarter of 2014. The number of home retention actions decreased 2.3 percent from the previous quarter and 32.1 percent from a year earlier. Servicers implemented 65,437 modifications, a decrease of 52.8 percent from a year earlier. New HAMP modifications increased 49.0 percent to 31,030 during the quarter, as program changes to FHA-HAMP materially increased the number of actions completed under the program. Other modifications decreased 33.4 percent from the previous quarter, to 34,407. Servicers implemented 71,381 new trial-period plans, a decrease of 13.2 percent from the previous quarter and 31.1 percent from a year earlier. New payment plans increased by 13.9 percent from the previous quarter to 100,315. During the past five quarters, servicers initiated 1.5 million home retention actions—483,940 modifications, 458,772 trial-period plans, and 515,492 payment plans.

	3/31/13	6/30/13	9/30/13	12/31/13	3/31/14	1Q %Change	1Y %Change
Table 13. Number of New Home Retention Actions							
Other Modifications	110,519	85,582	76,134	51,637	34,407	-33.4%	-68.9%
HAMP Modifications	28,030	22,613	23,159	20,829	31,030	49.0%	10.7%
Other Trial-Period Plans	85,516	68,465	62,163	50,743	48,321	-4.8%	-43.5%
HAMP Trial-Period Plans	18,145	32,028	38,804	31,527	23,060	-26.9%	27.1%
Payment Plans	107,113	107,403	112,568	88,093	100,315	13.9%	-6.3%
Total	349,323	316,091	312,828	242,829	237,133	-2.3%	-32.1%

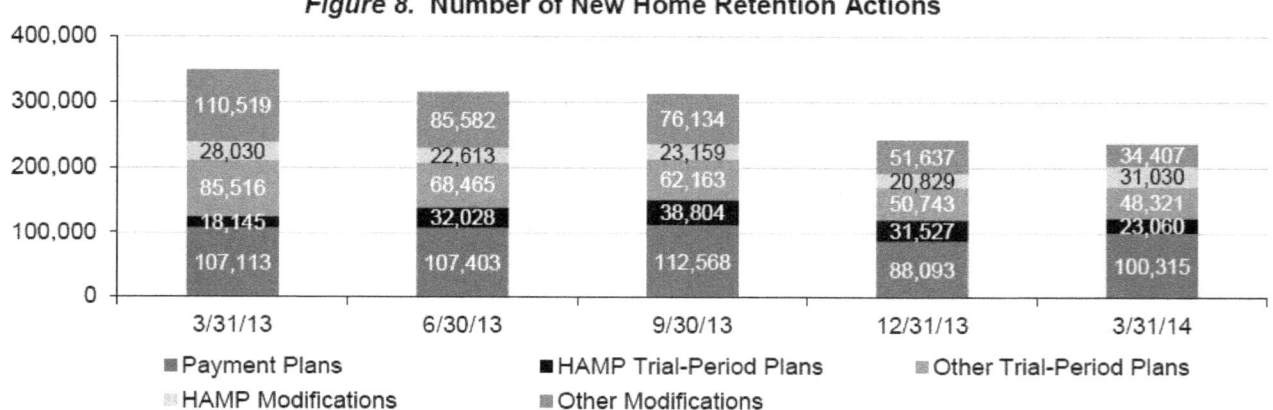

Figure 8. Number of New Home Retention Actions

HAMP Modifications and Trial-Period Plans, by Investor and Risk Category

Servicers implemented 31,030 HAMP modifications during the quarter, an increase of 10.7 percent from a year earlier. GSE mortgages received 11.9 percent of HAMP modifications completed during the quarter, government-guaranteed loans received 64.8 percent, loans held in portfolio received 12.8 percent, and loans serviced for private investors received 10.5 percent. Prime mortgages represented about 75 percent of the total portfolio and received 31.6 percent of all HAMP modifications. Subprime loans represented about 6 percent of the total portfolio and received 25.5 percent of HAMP modifications during the quarter.

Table 14. HAMP Modifications, by Investor and Risk Category						
(Modifications Implemented in the First Quarter of 2014)						
	Fannie Mae	Freddie Mac	Government-Guaranteed	Portfolio	Private	Total
Prime	860	1,138	4,921	1,651	1,244	9,814
Alt-A	268	330	6,794	973	782	9,147
Subprime	218	200	5,268	1,207	1,017	7,910
Other	478	195	3,117	150	219	4,159
Total	1,824	1,863	20,100	3,981	3,262	31,030

Servicers implemented 23,060 HAMP trial-period plans during the quarter, an increase of 27.1 percent from a year earlier. GSE mortgages received 10.7 percent of HAMP trial-period plans initiated during the quarter, government-guaranteed loans received 72.6 percent, loans held in portfolio received 7.3 percent, and loans serviced for private investors received 9.5 percent. Prime mortgages received 31.5 percent of the HAMP trial-period plans implemented during the quarter, Alt-A loans received 30.6 percent, and subprime and other mortgages collectively received 37.9 percent.

Table 15. HAMP Trial-Period Plans, by Investor and Risk Category						
(Trial-Period Plans Implemented in the First Quarter of 2014)						
	Fannie Mae	Freddie Mac	Government-Guaranteed	Portfolio	Private	Total
Prime	618	749	4,322	644	926	7,259
Alt-A	171	248	5,836	364	442	7,061
Subprime	140	120	4,099	515	688	5,562
Other	290	121	2,474	155	138	3,178
Total	1,219	1,238	16,731	1,678	2,194	23,060

New Home Retention Actions Relative to Newly Initiated Foreclosures

Servicers continued to implement more home retention actions than new foreclosures during the quarter. The ratio of new home retention actions to newly initiated foreclosures increased 33.3 percent from a year earlier. Although the number of new home retention actions and new foreclosures both decreased from the previous quarter and a year earlier, new retention actions fell less than new foreclosures.

Table 16. Percentage of New Home Retention Actions Relative to Newly Initiated Foreclosures, by Risk Category							
	3/31/13	6/30/13	9/30/13	12/31/13	3/31/14	1Q %Change	1Y %Change
Prime	216.0%	222.7%	246.7%	199.8%	266.2%	33.3%	23.3%
Alt-A	198.1%	216.6%	252.6%	209.6%	292.9%	39.7%	47.9%
Subprime	204.2%	212.6%	242.3%	190.1%	256.2%	34.8%	25.5%
Other	133.1%	163.9%	199.1%	169.3%	210.0%	24.1%	57.8%
Overall	195.9%	209.9%	239.5%	195.1%	261.0%	33.8%	33.3%
Number of New Home Retention Actions	349,323	316,091	312,828	242,829	237,133	-2.3%	-32.1%
Number of Newly Initiated Foreclosures	178,360	150,592	130,592	124,468	90,852	-27.0%	-49.1%

Figure 9. New Home Retention Actions Relative to Newly Initiated Foreclosures, by Risk Category

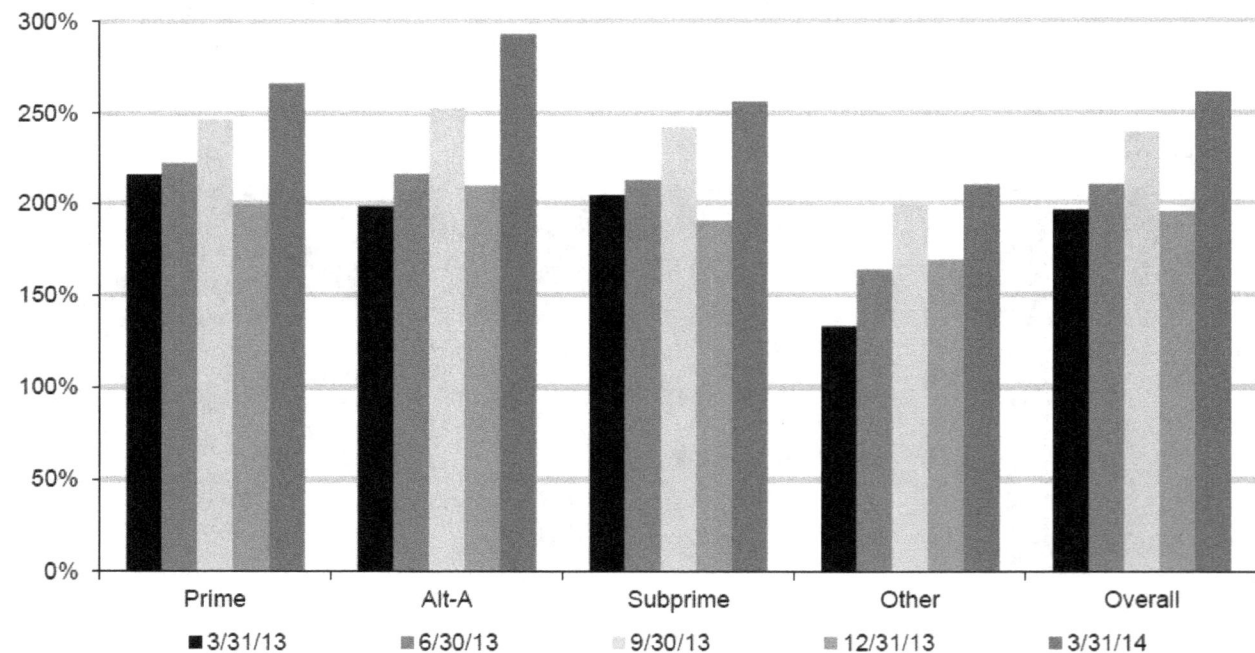

Types of Modification Actions

The types of modification actions or combinations of actions have different effects on the borrowers' mortgages and their monthly principal and interest payments. Different actions may have different effects on the long-term sustainability of mortgages. Servicers often use a combination of actions when modifying mortgages, with 92.8 percent of modifications implemented during the first quarter of 2014 changing more than one of the original loan terms. Capitalization, interest-rate reduction, and term extension remained the primary actions used in modifying mortgages.

Servicers capitalized missed fees and payments in 74.3 percent of modifications implemented during the quarter, reduced interest rates in 73.3 percent, and extended loan maturity in 78.0 percent. Servicers reduced some portion of the unpaid principal in 8.1 percent of modifications completed during the quarter, a decrease of 22.8 percent from the previous quarter and 46.4 percent from a year earlier. Servicers deferred repayment of some portion of the unpaid principal in 25.1 percent of modifications made during the quarter, up 37.8 percent from a year earlier. Because most modifications changed more than one term, the sum of the individual actions exceeded 100 percent of total modifications. Appendix D presents additional detail on combination modifications.

Table 17. Changes in Loan Terms for Modifications Through the First Quarter of 2014 (Percentage of Total Modifications in Each Category)							
	3/31/13	6/30/13	9/30/13	12/31/13	3/31/14	1Q %Change	1Y %Change
Capitalization	79.0%	81.6%	83.5%	87.7%	74.3%	-15.3%	-5.9%
Rate Reduction	80.1%	81.0%	78.9%	76.7%	73.3%	-4.4%	-8.5%
Rate Freeze	3.7%	5.2%	5.5%	7.0%	6.5%	-6.6%	76.9%
Term Extension	60.3%	67.7%	69.3%	75.9%	78.0%	2.7%	29.2%
Principal Reduction	15.2%	12.2%	13.6%	10.5%	8.1%	-22.8%	-46.4%
Principal Deferral	18.2%	20.5%	25.3%	30.6%	25.1%	-17.9%	37.8%
Not Reported*	0.7%	1.5%	2.2%	0.7%	0.7%	-5.6%	-1.7%
(Number of Changes in Each Category)							
Capitalization	109,418	88,240	82,894	63,545	48,625	-23.5%	-55.6%
Rate Reduction	110,910	87,639	78,309	55,554	47,939	-13.7%	-56.8%
Rate Freeze	5,121	5,619	5,413	5,072	4,279	-15.6%	-16.4%
Term Extension	83,594	73,254	68,820	55,026	51,030	-7.3%	-39.0%
Principal Reduction	21,033	13,150	13,502	7,634	5,322	-30.3%	-74.7%
Principal Deferral	25,272	22,195	25,150	22,195	16,450	-25.9%	-34.9%
Not Reported	933	1,571	2,191	508	433	-14.8%	-53.6%

*Processing constraints at some servicers have prevented them from reporting specific modified term(s). For example, servicers should report principal reduction actions in the month that the modification is first effective, but review indicates some have been reporting conditional reductions after the effective date of the modification. Data regarding principal reduction is expected to be revised upward as servicers correct reporting.

Types of HAMP Modification Actions

Consistent with modification actions overall and the prescribed order of actions required by the program, HAMP modifications most often included capitalization of missed payments and fees, interest-rate reductions, and term extensions. Servicers used capitalization in 51.0 percent of modifications, down from 93.9 percent a year ago. Servicers used term extension in 88.1 percent of modifications, up from 53.8 percent a year ago. Servicers used principal deferral, another prescribed action in HAMP, in 30.1 percent of HAMP modifications during the first quarter of 2014, down from 31.9 percent a year earlier. Servicers used principal reduction in 6.8 percent of HAMP modifications implemented during the quarter—a decrease of 56.3 percent from the previous quarter and 69.4 percent from a year earlier, when 22.3 percent of HAMP modifications included principal reduction.

Table 18. Changes in Loan Terms for HAMP Modifications Through the First Quarter of 2014 (Percentage of Total Modifications in Each Category)							
	3/31/13	6/30/13	9/30/13	12/31/13	3/31/14	1Q %Change	1Y %Change
Capitalization	93.9%	88.6%	90.3%	70.1%	51.0%	-27.2%	-45.6%
Rate Reduction	84.9%	88.8%	88.9%	90.3%	85.9%	-4.9%	1.2%
Rate Freeze	3.5%	2.6%	3.1%	2.4%	4.2%	76.2%	20.6%
Term Extension	53.8%	57.6%	60.1%	74.1%	88.1%	18.9%	63.7%
Principal Reduction	22.3%	20.0%	21.8%	15.6%	6.8%	-56.3%	-69.4%
Principal Deferral	31.9%	36.2%	35.0%	26.3%	30.1%	14.4%	-5.7%
Not Reported*	0.2%	0.4%	1.2%	0.3%	0.2%	-23.9%	37.3%
(Number of Changes in Each Category)							
Capitalization	26,308	20,027	20,912	14,591	15,830	8.5%	-39.8%
Rate Reduction	23,790	20,072	20,589	18,808	26,644	41.7%	12.0%
Rate Freeze	981	582	729	499	1,310	162.5%	33.5%
Term Extension	15,089	13,032	13,913	15,437	27,341	77.1%	81.2%
Principal Reduction	6,245	4,527	5,046	3,252	2,116	-34.9%	-66.1%
Principal Deferral	8,930	8,176	8,103	5,475	9,327	70.4%	4.4%
Not Reported	50	83	278	67	76	13.4%	52.0%

*See note to table 17.

Types of Modification Actions, by Risk Category

Servicers use a combination of actions when modifying mortgages. Modifications across all risk categories predominantly featured interest-rate reduction, term extension, and capitalization of past-due interest and fees. Because most modifications changed more than one term, the sum of individual features changed exceeded the total number of modified loans in each risk category. While servicers used most actions relatively consistently across all risk categories, servicers used principal deferral less frequently and principal reduction more often for subprime loans than for other risk classes.

Table 19. Changes in Loan Terms for Modifications, by Risk Category, During the First Quarter of 2014 (Percentage of Total Modifications in Each Category)					
	Prime	Alt-A	Subprime	Other	Overall
Capitalization	81.0%	65.9%	73.7%	71.6%	74.3%
Rate Reduction	72.7%	74.5%	73.0%	73.3%	73.3%
Rate Freeze	5.7%	6.0%	6.6%	10.1%	6.5%
Term Extension	77.5%	80.3%	72.3%	86.2%	78.0%
Principal Reduction	8.4%	7.8%	11.3%	1.4%	8.1%
Principal Deferral	26.0%	24.5%	21.9%	30.5%	25.1%
Not Reported*	0.9%	0.4%	0.5%	0.7%	0.7%
(Number of Changes in Each Category)					
Total Mortgages Modified	25,396	16,492	15,855	7,694	65,437
Capitalization	20,567	10,870	11,680	5,508	48,625
Rate Reduction	18,454	12,282	11,567	5,636	47,939
Rate Freeze	1,455	997	1,048	779	4,279
Term Extension	19,689	13,245	11,461	6,635	51,030
Principal Reduction	2,134	1,286	1,798	104	5,322
Principal Deferral	6,598	4,033	3,472	2,347	16,450
Not Reported	224	72	85	52	433

*See note to table 17.

Types of Modification Actions, by Investor and Product Type

Modifications of mortgages serviced for the GSEs accounted for 31.8 percent of all modifications made during the first quarter of 2014. Government-guaranteed loans received 36.8 percent of all modifications, mortgages serviced for private investors received 16.5 percent, and mortgages held in the servicers' own portfolios received 14.9 percent of all first-quarter modifications. Interest-rate reduction, capitalization of missed payments and fees, and term extension remained the primary types of modification actions. Servicers used principal reduction most frequently in modifying loans held in portfolio or serviced for private investors because Fannie Mae and Freddie Mac do not allow principal reduction. Because modifications often change more than one loan term, the sum of the actions exceeded the number of modified loans for each investor.

Table 20. Type of Modification Action, by Investor and Product Type, During the First Quarter of 2014 (Percentage of Total Modifications in Each Category)						
	Fannie Mae	Freddie Mac	Government-Guaranteed	Private Investor	Portfolio	Overall
Capitalization	76.0%	70.0%	36.5%	79.2%	93.6%	63.7%
Rate Reduction	56.8%	75.6%	82.8%	70.6%	69.5%	73.3%
Rate Freeze	9.6%	4.7%	6.6%	3.6%	7.8%	6.5%
Term Extension	90.0%	93.4%	96.1%	29.6%	57.8%	78.0%
Principal Reduction	0.0%	0.0%	0.1%	15.0%	37.6%	8.1%
Principal Deferral	20.8%	27.8%	22.3%	31.4%	27.6%	25.1%
Not Reported*	2.1%	0.3%	0.1%	1.9%	0.8%	0.9%
(Number of Changes in Each Category)						
Total Mortgages Modified	11,276	9,518	24,090	10,798	9,755	65,437
Capitalization	10,898	9,339	8,921	10,152	9,315	48,625
Rate Reduction	6,408	7,194	19,938	7,624	6,775	47,939
Rate Freeze	1,082	443	1,596	393	765	4,279
Term Extension	10,152	8,887	23,153	3,200	5,638	51,030
Principal Reduction	0**	0**	24	1,616	3,669	5,322
Principal Deferral	2,348	2,646	5,379	3,389	2,688	16,450
Not Reported	234	31	38	87	43	433

*See note to table 17.

**A negligible number of loans were miscoded as principal reduction for Fannie Mae and Freddie Mac and removed from reporting.

Types of HAMP Modification Actions, by Investor and Product Type

Of the 31,030 HAMP modifications implemented in the first quarter of 2014, 11.9 percent were on GSE mortgages, 64.8 percent were on government-guaranteed loans, 10.5 percent were on mortgages serviced for private investors, and 12.8 percent were on mortgages held in servicers' portfolios. Consistent with total modification actions, the prevailing actions among HAMP modifications were capitalization of past-due interest and fees, interest-rate reduction, and term extension. Servicers used principal deferral in a significant number of HAMP modifications for all investors. Principal reduction was concentrated in loans held in portfolio and serviced for private investors. More than 46 percent of the HAMP modifications completed during the first quarter of 2014 on loans held in the banks' own portfolios included a principal reduction.

Table 21. Type of HAMP Modification Action, by Investor and Product Type, During the First Quarter of 2014 (Percentage of Total Modifications in Each Category)						
	Fannie Mae	Freddie Mac	Government-Guaranteed	Private Investor	Portfolio	Overall
Capitalization	96.4%	98.8%	25.1%	99.5%	98.9%	51.0%
Rate Reduction	93.6%	99.1%	85.1%	83.0%	82.3%	85.9%
Rate Freeze	1.5%	1.0%	4.7%	3.8%	4.7%	4.2%
Term Extension	71.8%	72.8%	99.7%	47.6%	77.4%	88.1%
Principal Reduction	0.0%	0.0%	0.05%	7.8%	46.4%	6.8%
Principal Deferral	28.3%	30.9%	24.0%	64.5%	32.8%	30.1%
Not Reported*	2.1%	0.3%	0.1%	0.0%	0.0%	0.2%
(Number of Changes in Each Category)						
Total Mortgages Modified	1,824	1,863	20,100	3,262	3,981	31,030
Capitalization	1,758	1,841	5,050	3,245	3,936	15,830
Rate Reduction	1,708	1,846	17,106	2,709	3,275	26,644
Rate Freeze	27	18	952	124	189	1,310
Term Extension	1,310	1,356	20,041	1,552	3,082	27,341
Principal Reduction	0**	0	11	256	1,846	2,116
Principal Deferral	516	575	4,829	2,103	1,304	9,327
Not Reported	49	11	16	0	0	76

*See note to table 17.

**A negligible number of loans were miscoded as principal reduction for Fannie Mae and removed from reporting.

Changes in Monthly Payments Resulting From Modification

The previous sections of this report describe the types of modification actions across risk categories, investors, and product types. This section describes the effect of those changes on borrowers' monthly principal and interest payments.

Modifications that decrease payments occur when servicers elect to lower interest rates, extend the amortization period, or defer or forgive principal. The reduced payments can make mortgages more affordable to borrowers and more sustainable over time. The lower payments, however, also result in less monthly cash flow and interest income to mortgage investors.

Mortgage modifications may increase monthly payments when borrowers and servicers agree to add past-due interest, advances for taxes or insurance, and other fees to the loan balances and re-amortize the new balances over the remaining life of the mortgages. The interest rate or maturity of the loans may be changed on these modifications but not enough to offset the increase in payments caused by the additional capitalized principal. Modifications may also result in increased monthly payments when interest rates or principal payments on ARMs and payment-option ARMs are reset higher but by less than the amount indicated in the original mortgage contracts.

Modifications that increase payments may be appropriate when borrowers resolve temporary problems with cash flow, or otherwise have reasonable prospects of making higher payments to repay the debt over time. This strategy carries additional risk, however, especially during periods of prolonged economic stress, underscoring the importance of verifying borrowers' income and debt-payment ability so that borrowers and servicers have confidence that the modifications will be sustainable.

Servicers also modify some mortgage contracts by simply leaving principal and interest payments unchanged. This occurs, for example, when servicers "freeze" current interest rates and payments instead of allowing them to increase to levels required by the original mortgage contracts.

Changes in Monthly Payments Resulting From Modifications, by Quarter

Almost 91 percent of modifications made in the first quarter of 2014 reduced monthly principal and interest payments and 58.6 percent of the modifications reduced payments by 20 percent or more.

Table 22. Changes in Monthly Principal and Interest Payments Resulting From Modifications (Percentage of Modifications in Each Category)*							
	3/31/13	6/30/13	9/30/13	12/31/13	3/31/14	1Q %Change	1Y %Change
Decreased by 20% or More	56.4%	59.2%	62.5%	64.6%	58.6%	-9.2%	3.9%
Decreased by 10% to Less Than 20%	24.1%	21.4%	18.8%	16.9%	20.5%	21.2%	-15.1%
Decreased by Less Than 10%	13.2%	12.4%	11.1%	9.5%	11.8%	23.2%	-11.1%
Subtotal for Decreased	**93.7%**	**93.0%**	**92.4%**	**91.0%**	**90.8%**	**-0.2%**	**-3.1%**
Unchanged	0.9%	1.0%	0.8%	1.3%	1.8%	36.3%	97.7%
Increased	5.4%	6.0%	6.8%	7.7%	7.4%	-4.0%	37.7%
Subtotal for Unchanged and Increased	**6.3%**	**7.0%**	**7.6%**	**9.0%**	**9.2%**	**1.8%**	**46.3%**
Total	100.0%	100.0%	100.0%	100.0%	100.0%		
(Number of Modifications in Each Category)							
Decreased by 20% or More	77,674	63,515	61,308	46,511	38,026	-18.2%	-51.0%
Decreased by 10% to Less Than 20%	33,143	23,005	18,443	12,154	13,266	9.1%	-60.0%
Decreased by Less Than 10%	18,187	13,323	10,876	6,872	7,623	10.9%	-58.1%
Subtotal for Decreased	**129,004**	**99,843**	**90,627**	**65,537**	**58,915**	**-10.1%**	**-54.3%**
Unchanged	1,229	1,124	784	933	1,145	22.7%	-6.8%
Increased	7,389	6,405	6,643	5,550	4,796	-13.6%	-35.1%
Subtotal for Unchanged and Increased	**8,618**	**7,529**	**7,427**	**6,483**	**5,941**	**-8.4%**	**-31.1%**
Total	137,622	107,372	98,054	72,020	64,856	-9.9%	-52.9%

*No payment change information was reported on 927 modifications in the first quarter of 2013, 823 in the second quarter, 1,239 in the third quarter, 446 in the fourth quarter, and 581 in the first quarter of 2014.

Figure 10. Changes in Monthly Principal and Interest Payments
Percentage of Modifications in Each Category

■ Increased   ▩ Unchanged   ▨ Decreased

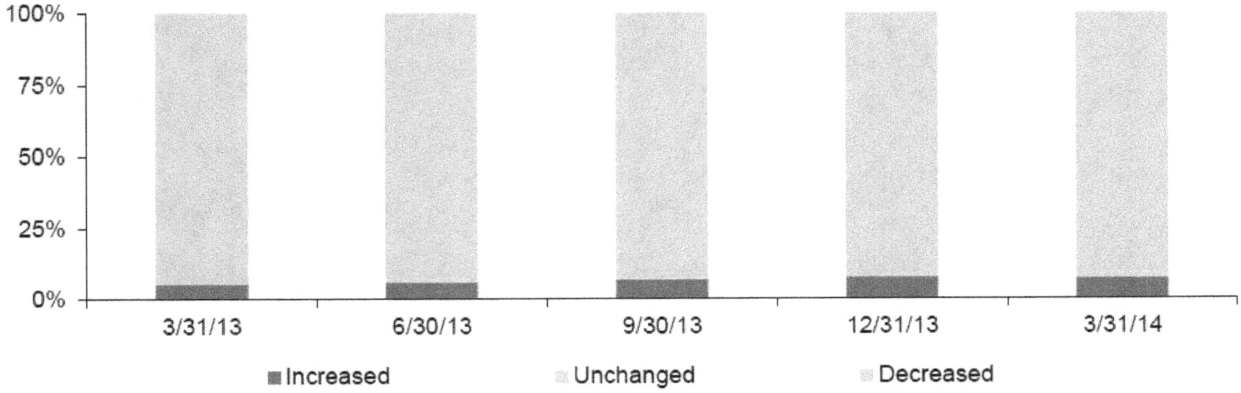

Changes in Monthly Payments Resulting From HAMP Modifications, by Quarter

Almost 99 percent of HAMP modifications completed during the first quarter of 2014 reduced borrower monthly payments, with 65.6 percent reducing payments by 20 percent or more. In addition to achieving lower payments, HAMP attempts to increase payment sustainability by targeting monthly payments at 31 percent of borrowers' income. Performance data on all modifications show that re-default rates are lowest among loans that receive at least a 10 percent reduction in their monthly payments, and that the greater the decrease in payment, the lower the rate of re-default.

Table 23. Changes in Monthly Principal and Interest Payments Resulting From HAMP Modifications (Percentage of HAMP Modifications in Each Category)*							
	3/31/13	6/30/13	9/30/13	12/31/13	3/31/14	1Q %Change	1Y %Change
Decreased by 20% or More	76.3%	77.8%	76.8%	73.7%	65.6%	-9.2%	3.9%
Decreased by 10% to Less Than 20%	13.1%	12.3%	13.4%	17.1%	23.2%	21.2%	-15.1%
Decreased by Less Than 10%	8.5%	7.4%	7.9%	7.3%	10.1%	23.2%	-11.1%
Subtotal for Decreased	**98.0%**	**97.5%**	**98.1%**	**98.1%**	**98.8%**	**-0.2%**	**-3.1%**
Unchanged	0.5%	0.9%	0.1%	0.1%	0.2%	36.3%	97.7%
Increased	1.5%	1.6%	1.8%	1.8%	1.0%	-4.0%	37.7%
Subtotal for Unchanged and Increased	**2.0%**	**2.5%**	**1.9%**	**1.9%**	**1.2%**	**1.8%**	**46.3%**
Total	100.0%	100.0%	100.0%	100.0%	100.0%		
(Number of HAMP Modifications in Each Category)							
Decreased by 20% or More	21,321	17,527	17,705	15,316	20,312	-18.2%	-51.0%
Decreased by 10% to Less Than 20%	3,672	2,768	3,088	3,554	7,176	9.1%	-60.0%
Decreased by Less Than 10%	2,389	1,671	1,817	1,508	3,116	10.9%	-58.1%
Subtotal for Decreased	**27,382**	**21,966**	**22,610**	**20,378**	**30,604**	**-10.1%**	**-54.3%**
Unchanged	138	205	34	25	60	22.7%	-6.8%
Increased	431	363	411	366	297	-13.6%	-35.1%
Subtotal for Unchanged and Increased	**569**	**568**	**445**	**391**	**357**	**-8.4%**	**-31.1%**
Total	27,951	22,534	23,055	20,769	30,961	-9.9%	-52.9%

*No payment change information was reported on 79 modifications in the first quarter of 2013, 79 in the second quarter, 104 in the third quarter, 60 in the fourth quarter, and 69 in the first quarter of 2014.

Average Change in Monthly Payments Resulting From Modifications, by Quarter

Modifications made during the first quarter of 2014 reduced monthly principal and interest payments by $292, or 23.8 percent, on average. HAMP modifications made during the quarter reduced payments by $312, or 27.1 percent, on average. Other modifications reduced payments by $275, or 20.8 percent, on average. The decrease in the average reduction in monthly payments can be attributed to the lower average balance of mortgages receiving modifications.

Table 24. Average Change in Monthly Payments Resulting From Modifications, by Quarter*							
All Modifications							
	3/31/13	6/30/13	9/30/13	12/31/13	3/31/14	1Q %Change	1Y %Change
Decreased by 20% or More	(560)	(545)	(535)	(498)	(449)	-9.8%	-19.8%
Decreased by 10% to Less Than 20%	(186)	(172)	(176)	(172)	(160)	-7.1%	-14.0%
Decreased by Less Than 10%	(71)	(68)	(67)	(68)	(63)	-6.9%	-11.4%
Unchanged	0	0	0	0	0		
Increased	166	159	159	161	148	-7.9%	-10.9%
Overall (in dollars)	(361)	(358)	(365)	(344)	(292)	-15.1%	-19.1%
Percentage Change	-25.2%	-25.9%	-26.6%	-26.6%	-23.8%		
Other Modifications							
Decreased by 20% or More	(516)	(503)	(492)	(483)	(485)	0.5%	-5.9%
Decreased by 10% to Less Than 20%	(183)	(167)	(170)	(171)	(179)	5.0%	-2.1%
Decreased by Less Than 10%	(70)	(66)	(65)	(66)	(64)	-3.1%	-9.1%
Unchanged	0	0	0	0	0		
Increased	165	158	158	161	149	-7.9%	-9.7%
Overall (in dollars)	(314)	(311)	(316)	(313)	(275)	-12.3%	-12.5%
Percentage Change	-22.7%	-23.4%	-24.2%	-24.5%	-20.8%		
HAMP Modifications							
Decreased by 20% or More	(677)	(654)	(642)	(527)	(417)	-21.0%	-38.4%
Decreased by 10% to Less Than 20%	(212)	(211)	(207)	(176)	(144)	-18.4%	-32.2%
Decreased by Less Than 10%	(77)	(79)	(78)	(74)	(62)	-16.9%	-19.5%
Unchanged	0	0	0	0	0		
Increased	193	183	171	152	140	-8.0%	-27.5%
Overall (in dollars)	(548)	(538)	(524)	(422)	(312)	-26.1%	-43.1%
Percentage Change	-35.0%	-35.1%	-34.6%	-31.5%	-27.1%		

*Parentheses indicate that, on average, borrowers' monthly payments decreased by the amount enclosed within the parentheses.

B. Modified Loan Performance

Re-Default Rates of Modified Loans: 60 or More Days Delinquent

Modification performance may vary because of many factors, including the types of modification actions, the average amount of change in the borrower's monthly payment, the characteristics and geographic location of the modified loans, and the addition or deletion of modification programs among the reporting institutions. Despite differences in many of these factors, mortgages modified in each of the last five quarters have performed similarly over time. Among modifications completed in each of the last five quarters, between 5.8 percent and 9.0 percent of the modified loans were 60 or more days delinquent three months after modification, while 16.9 percent to 18.5 percent were 60 or more days delinquent 12 months after modification.

Table 25. Modified Loans 60 or More Days Delinquent					
Modification Date*	3 Months After Modification	6 Months After Modification	9 Months After Modification	12 Months After Modification	15 Months After Modification
Fourth Quarter 2012	7.3%	11.5%	15.7%	18.5%	19.1%
First Quarter 2013	5.8%	11.6%	15.9%	16.9%	-
Second Quarter 2013	7.2%	13.6%	16.7%	-	-
Third Quarter 2013	9.0%	13.8%	-	-	-
Fourth Quarter 2013	7.1%	-	-	-	-

*All re-default data are based on modified loans that remain in effect at the specified amount of time after the modification. All loans that have been repaid in full, been refinanced, been sold, or completed the foreclosure process are removed from the calculation. Data include only modifications that have had time to age the indicated number of months.

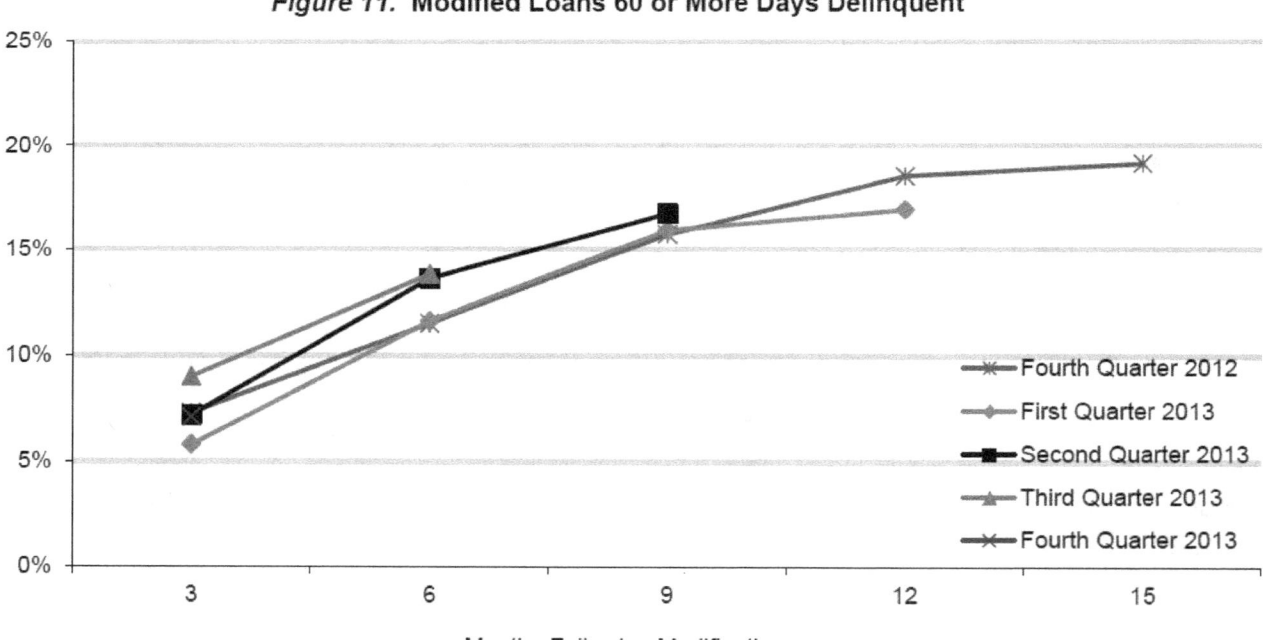

Figure 11. Modified Loans 60 or More Days Delinquent

Months Following Modification

*Data for the fourth quarter of 2013 is a single point (7.1 percent).

Re-Default Rates of Modified Loans: 30 or More Days Delinquent

Re-default rates measured at 30 or more days delinquent provide an early indicator of mortgages that may need additional attention to prevent more serious delinquency or foreclosure. For modifications completed in each of the last five quarters, 14.2 percent to 19.1 percent were 30 or more days delinquent three months after modification, while 26.0 to 28.5 percent were 30 or more days delinquent after one year.

Table 26. Modified Loans 30 or More Days Delinquent					
Modification Date*	3 Months After Modification	6 Months After Modification	9 Months After Modification	12 Months After Modification	15 Months After Modification
Fourth Quarter 2012	16.3%	21.3%	26.1%	28.5%	27.8%
First Quarter 2013	14.2%	22.1%	26.2%	26.0%	-
Second Quarter 2013	17.4%	24.9%	26.7%	-	-
Third Quarter 2013	19.1%	24.1%	-	-	-
Fourth Quarter 2013	16.9%	-	-	-	-

*Data include only modifications that have had time to age the indicated number of months.

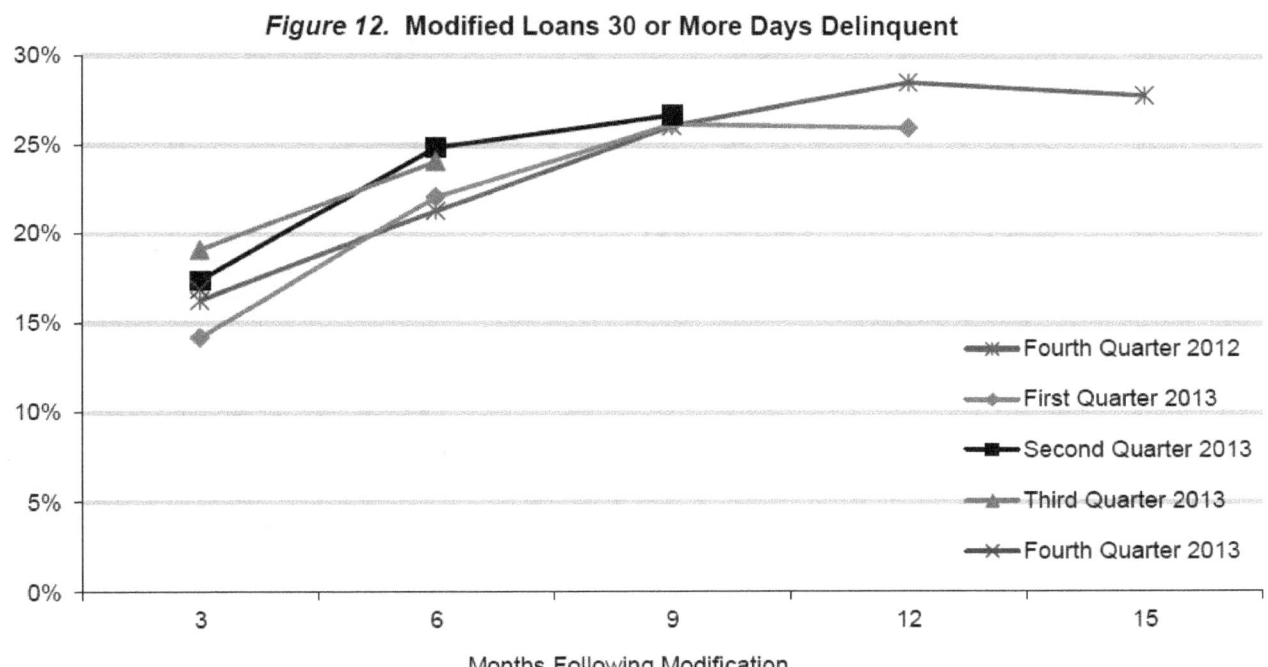

Figure 12. Modified Loans 30 or More Days Delinquent

*Data for the fourth quarter of 2013 is a single point (16.9 percent).

Re-Default Rates of Modified Loans: 90 or More Days Delinquent

Among modifications completed during the last five quarters, 12.5 percent to 13.4 percent were 90 or more days delinquent 12 months after modification.

Modification Date*	3 Months After Modification	6 Months After Modification	9 Months After Modification	12 Months After Modification	15 Months After Modification
Fourth Quarter 2012	3.7%	7.1%	10.7%	13.4%	14.7%
First Quarter 2013	2.7%	6.9%	10.6%	12.5%	-
Second Quarter 2013	3.2%	8.3%	11.5%	-	-
Third Quarter 2013	4.8%	8.9%	-	-	-
Fourth Quarter 2013	3.4%	-	-	-	-

Table 27. Modified Loans 90 or More Days Delinquent*

*Data include only modifications that have had time to age the indicated number of months.

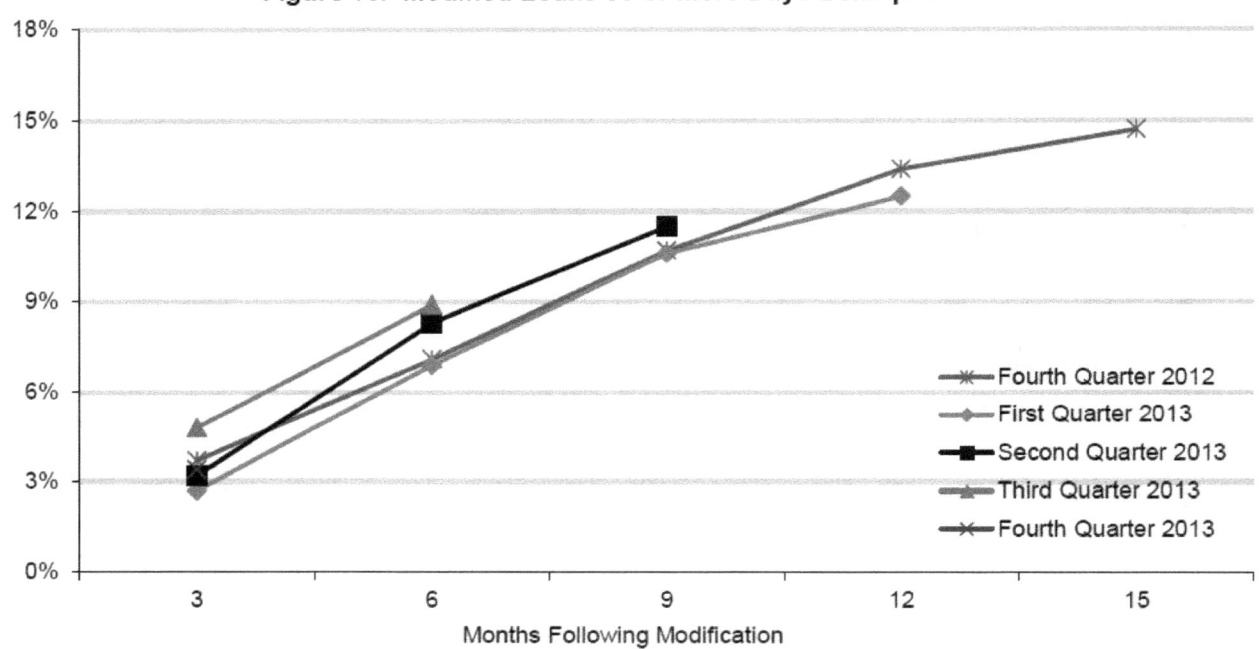

Figure 13. Modified Loans 90 or More Days Delinquent

*Data for the fourth quarter of 2013 is a single point (3.4 percent).

Re-Default Rate, by Investor (60 or More Days Delinquent)

Modifications on mortgages held in the servicers' own portfolios have performed better than modifications on mortgages serviced for other investors. Performance on mortgages serviced for other investors varies by investor and the year that a loan was modified. These re-default rates reflect differences in loan risk characteristics and modification programs. For all investors, re-default rates generally have decreased over time as more recent modifications have focused more on reducing monthly payments and increasing borrowers' ability to sustain the reduced payments over time and as the housing market and broader economy have continued their recovery.

Table 28. Re-Default Rates for Portfolio Loans and Loans Serviced for Others Modified in 2008
(60 or More Days Delinquent)

Investor Loan Type	6 Months After Modification	12 Months After Modification	18 Months After Modification	24 Months After Modification	36 Months After Modification
Fannie Mae	45.2%	59.7%	63.9%	62.2%	54.4%
Freddie Mac	45.0%	59.2%	64.4%	64.6%	59.5%
Government-Guaranteed	53.6%	67.8%	70.8%	70.3%	67.7%
Private	49.1%	61.2%	66.7%	68.0%	68.2%
Portfolio Loans	25.2%	36.2%	41.0%	41.7%	40.1%
Overall	44.8%	57.2%	62.1%	62.7%	61.4%

Table 29. Re-Default Rates for Portfolio Loans and Loans Serviced for Others Modified in 2009
(60 or More Days Delinquent)

Investor Loan Type	6 Months After Modification	12 Months After Modification	18 Months After Modification	24 Months After Modification	36 Months After Modification
Fannie Mae	31.3%	41.1%	42.5%	42.4%	39.1%
Freddie Mac	37.3%	44.8%	46.0%	44.9%	40.1%
Government-Guaranteed	42.1%	55.6%	56.4%	56.3%	58.6%
Private	40.8%	52.5%	56.8%	57.8%	54.4%
Portfolio Loans	15.4%	24.9%	29.6%	30.6%	30.2%
Overall	32.2%	43.2%	46.4%	46.9%	45.1%

Table 30. Re-Default Rates for Portfolio Loans and Loans Serviced for Others Modified in 2010
(60 or More Days Delinquent)

Investor Loan Type	6 Months After Modification	12 Months After Modification	18 Months After Modification	24 Months After Modification	36 Months After Modification
Fannie Mae	14.2%	20.6%	23.9%	24.3%	23.2%
Freddie Mac	12.1%	17.8%	20.7%	21.9%	20.8%
Government-Guaranteed	27.4%	40.7%	46.6%	48.8%	49.1%
Private	19.8%	28.3%	33.2%	33.7%	29.0%
Portfolio Loans	11.7%	18.0%	20.9%	22.0%	20.9%
Overall	17.3%	25.4%	29.5%	30.6%	29.2%

Table 31. Re-Default Rates for Portfolio Loans and Loans Serviced for Others Modified in 2011
(60 or More Days Delinquent)*

Investor Loan Type	6 Months After Modification	12 Months After Modification	18 Months After Modification	24 Months After Modification	36 Months After Modification
Fannie Mae	11.2%	16.7%	18.9%	20.4%	19.3%
Freddie Mac	10.9%	16.8%	20.1%	19.3%	19.4%
Government-Guaranteed	28.0%	42.3%	47.9%	48.1%	45.7%
Private	15.5%	22.1%	24.5%	21.5%	22.8%
Portfolio Loans	9.3%	15.1%	18.1%	18.1%	14.9%
Overall	15.4%	23.2%	26.6%	26.4%	26.6%

Table 32. Re-Default Rates for Portfolio Loans and Loans Serviced for Others Modified in 2012
(60 or More Days Delinquent)*

Investor Loan Type	6 Months After Modification	12 Months After Modification	18 Months After Modification	24 Months After Modification	36 Months After Modification
Fannie Mae	11.5%	16.9%	20.7%	20.9%	-
Freddie Mac	8.8%	12.9%	14.5%	13.8%	-
Government-Guaranteed	21.3%	33.4%	38.8%	40.0%	-
Private	13.0%	16.8%	15.8%	13.2%	-
Portfolio Loans	7.2%	11.1%	13.3%	20.8%	-
Overall	12.7%	18.8%	21.1%	21.5%	-

Table 33. Re-Default Rates for Portfolio Loans and Loans Serviced for Others Modified in 2013
(60 or More Days Delinquent)*

Investor Loan Type	6 Months After Modification	12 Months After Modification	18 Months After Modification	24 Months After Modification	36 Months After Modification
Fannie Mae	12.0%	16.6%	-	-	-
Freddie Mac	9.0%	12.3%	-	-	-
Government-Guaranteed	18.7%	26.5%	-	-	-
Private	11.5%	12.2%	-	-	-
Portfolio Loans	8.1%	9.4%	-	-	-
Overall	12.8%	16.9%	-	-	-

*Data in tables 31-33 include modifications that were originated that year and aged the indicated number of months.

Performance of HAMP Modifications Compared With Other Modifications

HAMP modifications have performed better than other modifications implemented during the same periods. These lower post-modification delinquency rates reflect HAMP's emphasis on the affordability of monthly payments relative to the borrower's income, verification of income, and completion of a successful trial-payment period. While these criteria result in better performance of HAMP modifications over time, the greater flexibility in making other types of modifications results in more of those modifications for borrowers who do not qualify for HAMP modifications.

Table 34. Performance of HAMP Modifications Compared With Other Modifications						
(60 or More Days Delinquent)*						
	Number of Modifications	3 Months After Modification	6 Months After Modification	9 Months After Modification	12 Months After Modification	15 Months After Modification
HAMP First Quarter 2012	37,240	4.9%	8.4%	11.3%	13.0%	13.3%
Other First Quarter 2012	65,861	9.4%	17.5%	23.1%	25.5%	25.5%
HAMP Second Quarter 2012	28,627	4.4%	7.9%	10.1%	11.0%	12.0%
Other Second Quarter 2012	68,088	7.5%	14.5%	17.9%	19.4%	19.4%
HAMP Third Quarter 2012	31,745	4.3%	7.7%	9.4%	11.0%	12.3%
Other Third Quarter 2012	104,764	8.0%	14.6%	17.9%	21.2%	21.2%
HAMP Fourth Quarter 2012	29,314	3.8%	6.2%	8.7%	10.3%	11.4%
Other Fourth Quarter 2012	114,181	8.3%	12.8%	17.5%	20.6%	20.6%
HAMP First Quarter 2013	28,030	3.2%	6.4%	8.9%	10.3%	-
Other First Quarter 2013	110,519	6.5%	13.0%	17.7%	18.6%	-
HAMP Second Quarter 2013	22,613	3.4%	6.9%	8.9%	-	-
Other Second Quarter 2013	85,582	8.3%	15.4%	18.8%	-	-
HAMP Third Quarter 2013	23,159	3.9%	7.0%	-	-	-
Other Third Quarter 2013	76,134	10.6%	15.9%	-	-	-
HAMP Fourth Quarter 2013	20,829	3.7%	-	-	-	-
Other Fourth Quarter 2013	51,637	8.5%	-	-	-	-

*Data include all modifications that have had time to age the indicated number of months.

C. Modified Loan Performance, by Change in Monthly Payments

Modifications that reduce borrowers' monthly payments by at least 10 percent consistently re-default at lower rates than those of other modifications—the larger the reduction in monthly payment, the lower the subsequent re-default rate. Lower re-default rates also may result from monthly payments set relative to the borrower's ability to repay, as well as verification of income and completion of a successful trial period.

For servicers and investors, determining the best type of modification often requires weighing the reduction in cash flow from reducing monthly principal and interest payments and the possible costs of delaying foreclosure, against the potential for longer-term sustainability of the payments and ultimate repayment of the mortgage.

Re-Default Rates of Loans by Change in Payment

Tables 35 through 40 present re-default rates, measured as 60 or more days delinquent, for modifications made since January 1, 2008. Data show that re-default rates decrease as reductions in payments increase more than 10 percent. Modification performance has improved over time as modifications focused on substantively reducing monthly payments and setting payments relative to the borrower's income and ability to pay.

For modifications completed in 2010, 2011, and 2012, actions that resulted in no change to the borrower's monthly payment have performed better than some modifications that reduced payments. Modifications that do not change monthly payment generally freeze the interest rate on an ARM so that rate and payment do not increase. These actions often are offered to borrowers who are current on their payments.

Table 35. Re-Default Rates of Loans Modified in 2008 by Change in Payment (60 or More Days Delinquent)					
	6 Months After Modification	12 Months After Modification	18 Months After Modification	24 Months After Modification	36 Months After Modification
Decreased by 20% or More	26.1%	39.6%	47.0%	49.1%	50.6%
Decreased by 10% to Less Than 20%	32.7%	47.5%	54.3%	55.6%	54.9%
Decreased by Less Than 10%	40.3%	55.2%	60.6%	61.0%	59.0%
Unchanged	53.7%	62.2%	66.3%	67.2%	65.8%
Increased	53.6%	67.3%	71.3%	71.1%	68.3%
Total	44.5%	57.0%	62.0%	62.7%	61.4%

Table 36. Re-Default Rates of Loans Modified in 2009 by Change in Payment (60 or More Days Delinquent)					
	6 Months After Modification	12 Months After Modification	18 Months After Modification	24 Months After Modification	36 Months After Modification
Decreased by 20% or More	19.2%	28.5%	32.8%	34.3%	33.6%
Decreased by 10% to Less Than 20%	29.2%	41.6%	45.0%	45.7%	45.4%
Decreased by Less Than 10%	33.8%	46.7%	49.3%	49.6%	49.9%
Unchanged	48.6%	57.3%	60.8%	61.4%	57.3%
Increased	46.5%	60.0%	62.5%	62.1%	58.6%
Total	32.2%	43.2%	46.5%	47.0%	45.1%

Table 37. Re-Default Rates of Loans Modified in 2010 by Change in Payment (60 or More Days Delinquent)*

	6 Months After Modification	12 Months After Modification	18 Months After Modification	24 Months After Modification	36 Months After Modification
Decreased by 20% or More	11.4%	17.4%	21.1%	22.3%	21.5%
Decreased by 10% to Less Than 20%	19.8%	30.3%	35.6%	37.3%	37.0%
Decreased by Less Than 10%	26.1%	37.4%	42.7%	43.9%	42.8%
Unchanged	18.8%	23.0%	24.8%	24.1%	20.6%
Increased	32.8%	44.1%	48.1%	48.8%	45.0%
Total	17.3%	25.4%	29.5%	30.6%	29.2%

Table 38. Re-Default Rates of Loans Modified in 2011 by Change in Payment (60 or More Days Delinquent)*

	6 Months After Modification	12 Months After Modification	18 Months After Modification	24 Months After Modification	36 Months After Modification
Decreased by 20% or More	9.5%	14.8%	17.5%	17.4%	18.6%
Decreased by 10% to Less Than 20%	16.7%	26.6%	31.2%	31.7%	33.5%
Decreased by Less Than 10%	22.7%	34.3%	38.9%	38.3%	32.4%
Unchanged	13.5%	17.3%	18.5%	17.7%	15.5%
Increased	32.8%	44.9%	49.7%	49.0%	46.6%
Total	15.4%	23.2%	26.6%	26.4%	26.6%

Table 39. Re-Default Rates of Loans Modified in 2012 by Change in Payment (60 or More Days Delinquent)*

	6 Months After Modification	12 Months After Modification	18 Months After Modification	24 Months After Modification	36 Months After Modification
Decreased by 20% or More	8.8%	13.2%	14.9%	15.1%	-
Decreased by 10% to Less Than 20%	12.5%	19.5%	22.4%	26.1%	-
Decreased by Less Than 10%	22.1%	33.3%	37.4%	36.5%	-
Unchanged	9.9%	11.3%	11.6%	29.3%	-
Increased	29.0%	38.8%	42.0%	39.2%	-
Total	12.7%	18.8%	21.1%	21.5%	-

Table 40. Re-Default Rates of Loans Modified in 2013 by Change in Payment (60 or More Days Delinquent)*

	6 Months After Modification	12 Months After Modification	18 Months After Modification	24 Months After Modification	36 Months After Modification
Decreased by 20% or More	9.0%	12.1%	-	-	-
Decreased by 10% to Less Than 20%	14.4%	18.4%	-	-	-
Decreased by Less Than 10%	21.7%	28.7%	-	-	-
Unchanged	20.0%	23.0%	-	-	-
Increased	24.2%	28.3%	-	-	-
Total	12.8%	16.9%	-	-	-

*Data in tables 38-40 include modifications that were originated that year and aged the indicated number of months.

60+ Delinquency at Six Months After Modification by Change in Monthly Payment

Modifications that reduced monthly principal and interest payments by at least 10 percent consistently performed better than other modifications. Modifications with the greatest decrease in monthly payments consistently had the lowest re-default rates. Some modifications that resulted in no change to the borrowers' monthly payments have performed better than modifications that reduced payments because these modifications likely were offered to borrowers with ARMs who had not defaulted on their payments.

Table 41. 60+ Delinquency at Six Months After Modification by Change in Monthly Payment						
	Decreased by 20% or More	Decreased by 10% to Less Than 20%	Decreased by Less Than 10%	Unchanged	Increased	Overall
Third Quarter 2012	8.7%	12.6%	23.3%	7.3%	30.8%	13.0%
Fourth Quarter 2012	8.0%	11.9%	20.1%	20.5%	23.6%	11.4%
First Quarter 2013	8.2%	12.1%	19.8%	21.0%	22.5%	11.6%
Second Quarter 2013	9.2%	15.8%	23.5%	18.1%	27.1%	13.6%
Third Quarter 2013	9.9%	17.1%	22.9%	21.3%	23.3%	13.7%
Total for the quarters above	8.7%	13.4%	21.7%	12.3%	25.6%	12.5%

Figure 14. 60+ Delinquency at Six Months After Modification by Change in Monthly Payment

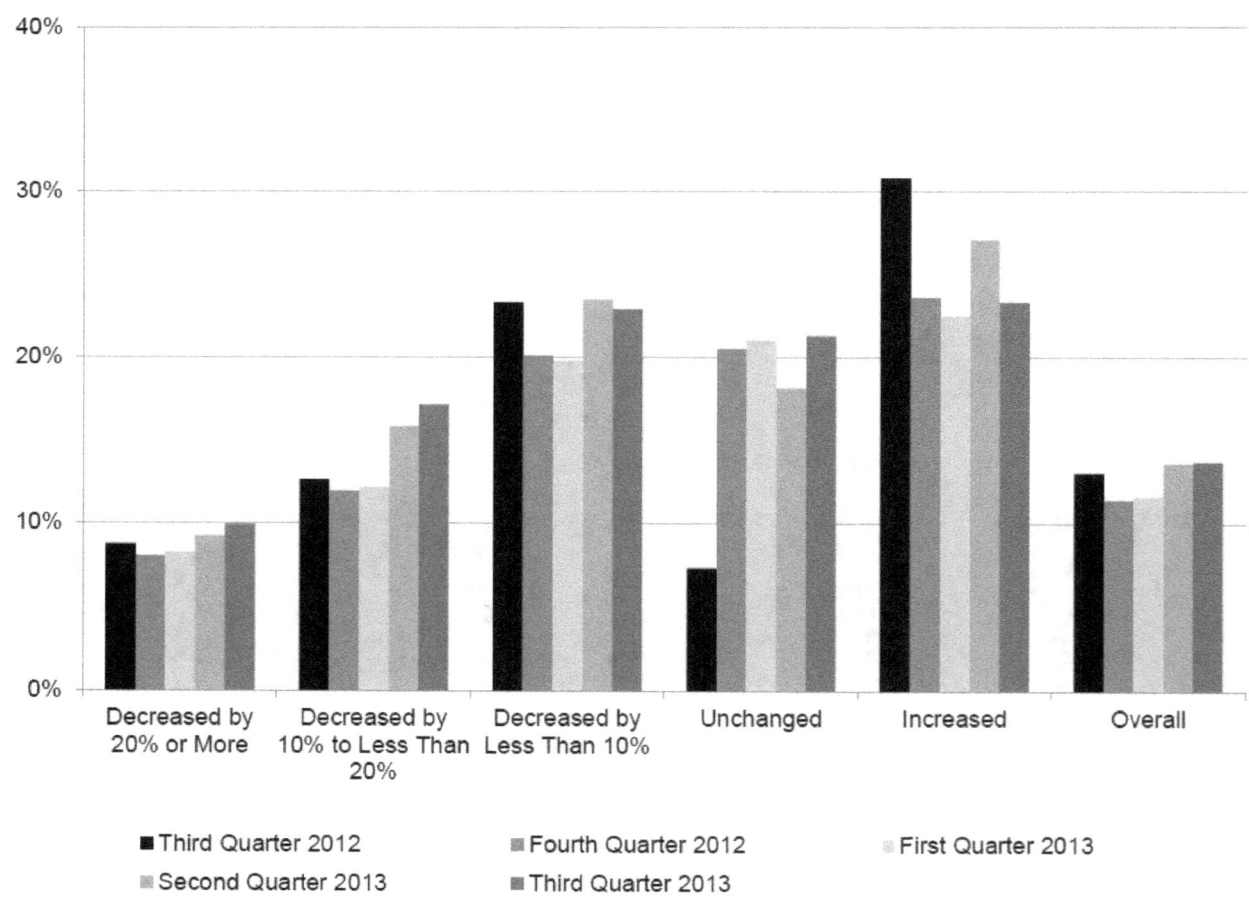

Status of Mortgages Modified in 2008–4Q 2013

Servicers implemented 3,460,476 modifications from January 1, 2008, through December 31, 2013. Of these modifications, 60 percent were active at the end of the first quarter of 2014 and 40 percent had exited the portfolios of the reporting institutions, through payment in full, involuntary liquidation—completed foreclosure, short sale or deed-in-lieu—or transfer to a non-reporting servicer. Of the 2,071,078 modifications that were active at the end of the first quarter of 2014, 69.9 percent were current and performing at quarter end, 23.9 percent were delinquent, and 6.1 percent were in the process of foreclosure. Among the 40 percent of modifications that had exited the portfolio prior to the end of the first quarter of 2014, 8.2 percent had been liquidated involuntarily, through foreclosure, short sale, or deed-in-lieu. Another 3.3 percent had been paid in full, and 28.7 percent had been transferred. HAMP modifications implemented since the third quarter of 2009 have performed better than other modifications. Modifications that reduced borrowers' monthly payments by 10 percent or more performed significantly better than other modifications. Of the 1,413,535 modifications that reduced payments by 10 percent or more and were active at the end of the first quarter of 2014, 74.7 percent were current, compared with 59.7 percent of modifications that reduced payments by less than 10 percent.

Table 42. Status of Mortgages Modified in 2008–4Q 2013

Year	Completed Modifications		As Percent of Modifications Active as of 3/31/14				As Percent of All Modifications Completed		
	Total	Active at 3/31/14	Current	30–59 Days Delinquent	Seriously Delinquent	Foreclosures in Process	Completed Foreclosures IL*	Paid Off	No Longer in the Portfolio
2008	443,294	147,566	59.5%	9.4%	21.1%	10.0%	17.3%	4.9%	44.5%
2009	593,884	276,567	63.0%	8.6%	19.6%	8.7%	13.6%	4.8%	35.1%
2010	955,422	536,606	68.7%	8.0%	16.4%	6.9%	9.2%	3.8%	30.9%
2011	569,553	371,910	70.1%	7.7%	15.8%	6.4%	4.9%	3.0%	26.7%
2012	479,820	374,635	73.8%	7.5%	13.9%	4.8%	1.6%	1.9%	18.5%
2013	418,503	363,794	77.0%	8.5%	11.8%	2.7%	0.3%	0.8%	12.0%
Total	3,460,476	2,071,078	69.9%	8.1%	15.8%	6.1%	8.2%	3.3%	28.7%
HAMP Modification Performance Compared With Other Modifications*									
HAMP	781,872	502,478	80.9%	6.3%	9.0%	3.8%	3.7%	2.0%	30.1%
Other**	1,897,464	1,280,979	67.8%	8.6%	17.4%	6.3%	6.9%	3.3%	22.3%
Modifications That Reduced Payments by 10 Percent or More									
	2,222,103	1,413,535	74.7%	7.6%	12.8%	4.9%	5.6%	2.5%	28.3%
Modifications That Reduced Payments by Less Than 10 Percent									
	1,238,373	657,543	59.7%	9.2%	22.2%	8.9%	12.8%	4.9%	29.3%

*Completed foreclosures or other involuntarily liquidated mortgages.

**Modifications used to compare with HAMP modifications only include modifications implemented from the third quarter of 2009 through the fourth quarter of 2013.

Part III: Home Forfeiture Actions—Foreclosures, Short Sales, and Deed-in-Lieu-of-Foreclosure Actions

Completed Foreclosures and Other Home Forfeiture Actions

Home forfeiture actions—completed foreclosure sales, short sales, and deed-in-lieu-of-foreclosure actions—totaled 71,678 during the first quarter of 2014, a decrease of 45.6 percent from a year earlier. The number of completed foreclosures decreased to 56,185—down 7.5 percent from the previous quarter and 33.9 percent from a year earlier. Short sales decreased 35.6 percent from the previous quarter and 68.4 percent from a year earlier. Short sales were 19.0 percent of total home forfeiture actions, down from 32.8 percent a year earlier. Deed-in-lieu-of-foreclosure actions remained a small portion of home forfeiture actions during the quarter.

Table 43. Completed Foreclosures and Other Home Forfeiture Actions							
	3/31/13	6/30/13	9/30/13	12/31/13	3/31/14	1Q %Change	1Y %Change
Completed Foreclosures	84,977	79,960	82,841	60,765	56,185	-7.5%	-33.9%
New Short Sales	43,143	39,207	31,261	21,149	13,613	-35.6%	-68.4%
New Deed-in-Lieu-of-Foreclosure Actions	3,596	2,579	2,112	2,117	1,880	-11.2%	-47.7%
Total	131,716	121,746	116,214	84,031	71,678	-14.7%	-45.6%

Newly Initiated Foreclosures

Servicers initiate foreclosure actions at defined stages of loan delinquency. Foreclosure actions progress to sale of the property only if servicers and borrowers cannot arrange a permanent loss mitigation action, modification, home sale, or alternate workout solution. Newly initiated foreclosures decreased to 90,852 in the first quarter of 2014, a decrease of 27.0 percent from the previous quarter and 49.1 percent from a year earlier.

Table 44. Number of Newly Initiated Foreclosures							
	3/31/13	6/30/13	9/30/13	12/31/13	3/31/14	1Q %Change	1Y %Change
Prime	72,198	61,405	52,211	49,420	35,678	-27.8%	-50.6%
Alt-A	38,052	32,749	29,287	27,910	20,435	-26.8%	-46.3%
Subprime	38,464	32,667	28,491	27,820	20,181	-27.5%	-47.5%
Other	29,646	23,771	20,603	19,318	14,558	-24.6%	-50.9%
Total	178,360	150,592	130,592	124,468	90,852	-27.0%	-49.1%

Figure 15. Number of Newly Initiated Foreclosures

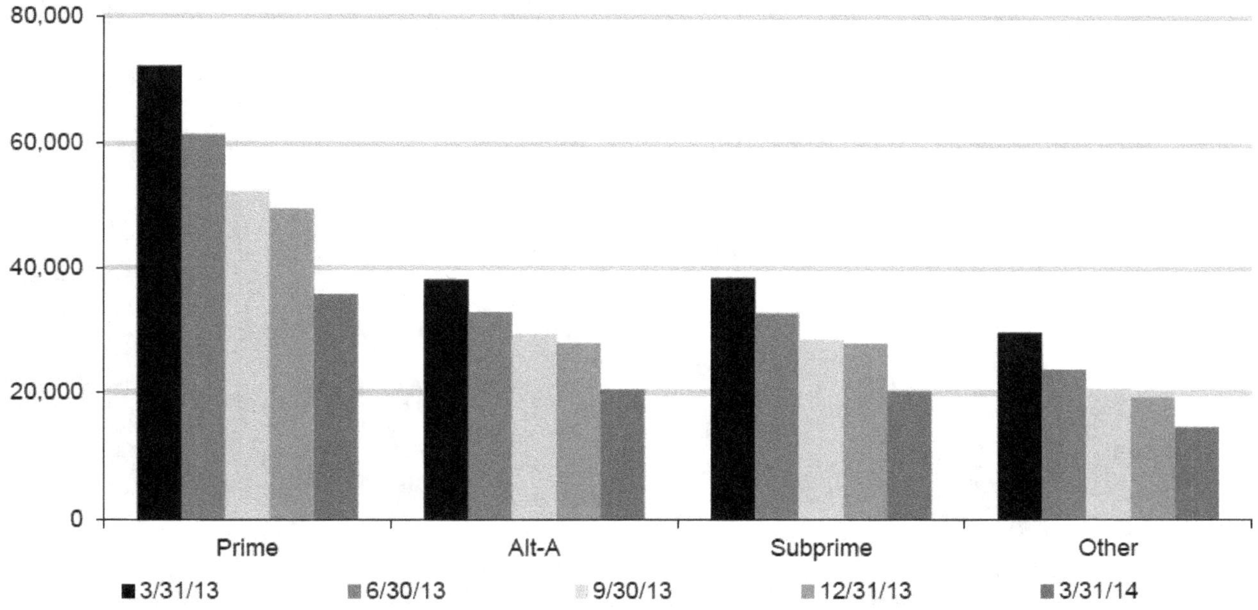

Foreclosures in Process

The number of mortgages in the process of foreclosure decreased to 432,832 at the end of the first quarter of 2014, down 17.3 percent from the previous quarter and 52.3 percent from a year earlier. The percentage of mortgages in the portfolio that were in some stage of the foreclosure process at the end of the first quarter of 2014 was 1.8 percent, a decrease of 16.0 percent from the previous quarter and 45.6 percent from a year earlier.

Table 45. Foreclosures in Process							
Percentage of Foreclosures in Process Relative to Mortgages in That Risk Category							
	3/31/13	6/30/13	9/30/13	12/31/13	3/31/14	1Q %Change	1Y %Change
Prime	1.9%	1.6%	1.3%	1.2%	1.0%	-17.2%	-48.7%
Alt-A	6.0%	5.3%	4.6%	4.2%	3.6%	-14.0%	-39.2%
Subprime	10.5%	9.3%	8.0%	7.3%	6.4%	-12.8%	-39.4%
Other	5.0%	4.6%	4.0%	3.7%	3.1%	-15.8%	-37.1%
Total	3.2%	2.8%	2.4%	2.1%	1.8%	-16.0%	-45.6%
Number of Foreclosures in Process							
Prime	390,415	316,235	255,583	221,675	181,465	-18.1%	-53.5%
Alt-A	179,261	148,632	122,232	107,033	90,308	-15.6%	-49.6%
Subprime	200,731	162,774	130,037	111,260	93,286	-16.2%	-53.5%
Other	136,821	116,728	96,911	83,560	67,773	-18.9%	-50.5%
Total	907,228	744,369	604,763	523,528	432,832	-17.3%	-52.3%

Figure 16. **Number of Foreclosures in Process**

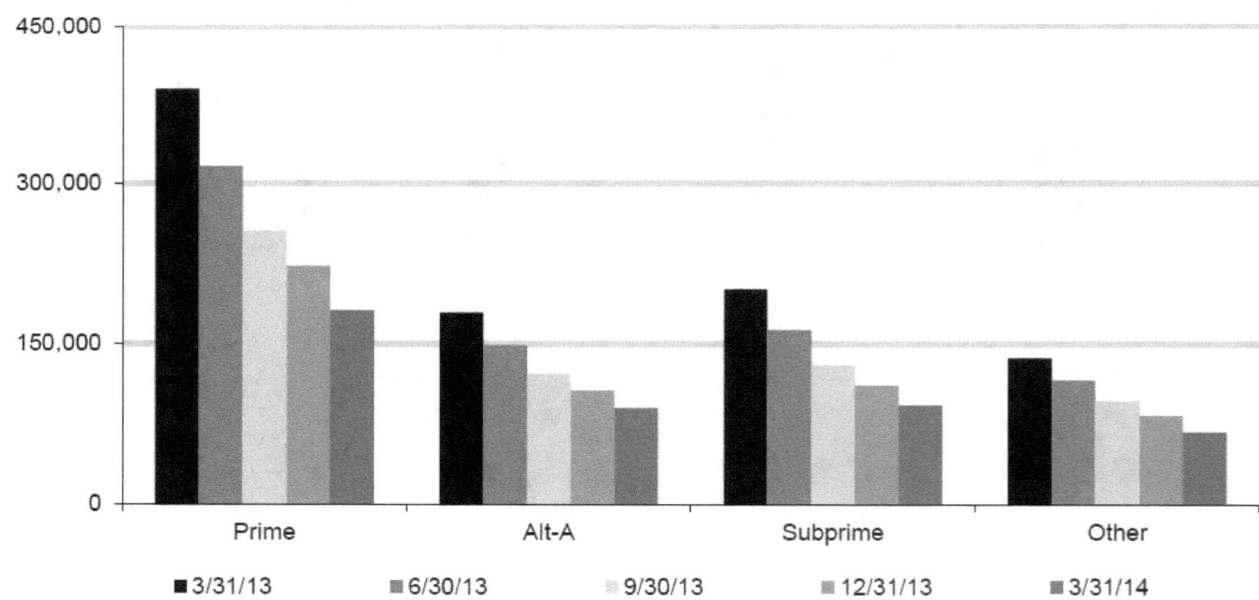

Completed Foreclosures

The number of completed foreclosures was 56,185 during the first quarter of 2014—a decrease of 7.5 percent from the previous quarter and 33.9 percent from a year earlier. The percentage of mortgages that completed the foreclosure process during the first quarter of 2014 was 0.2 percent of all mortgages serviced, a decrease of 6.0 percent from the previous quarter and 24.6 percent from a year earlier.

	3/31/13	6/30/13	9/30/13	12/31/13	3/31/14	1Q %Change	1Y %Change
Table 46. Completed Foreclosures							
Percentage of Completed Foreclosures Relative to Mortgages in That Risk Category							
Prime	0.2%	0.2%	0.2%	0.1%	0.1%	-5.7%	-33.8%
Alt-A	0.5%	0.6%	0.6%	0.5%	0.5%	-5.5%	-13.3%
Subprime	0.9%	1.0%	1.1%	0.8%	0.8%	-7.0%	-9.3%
Other	0.5%	0.5%	0.6%	0.5%	0.4%	-2.4%	-7.2%
Total	0.3%	0.3%	0.3%	0.2%	0.2%	-6.0%	-24.6%
Number of Completed Foreclosures							
Prime	39,255	34,686	33,817	25,253	23,547	-6.8%	-40.0%
Alt-A	16,005	15,943	17,062	12,410	11,502	-7.3%	-28.1%
Subprime	16,588	16,654	17,992	12,902	11,539	-10.6%	-30.4%
Other	13,129	12,677	13,970	10,200	9,597	-5.9%	-26.9%
Total	84,977	79,960	82,841	60,765	56,185	-7.5%	-33.9%

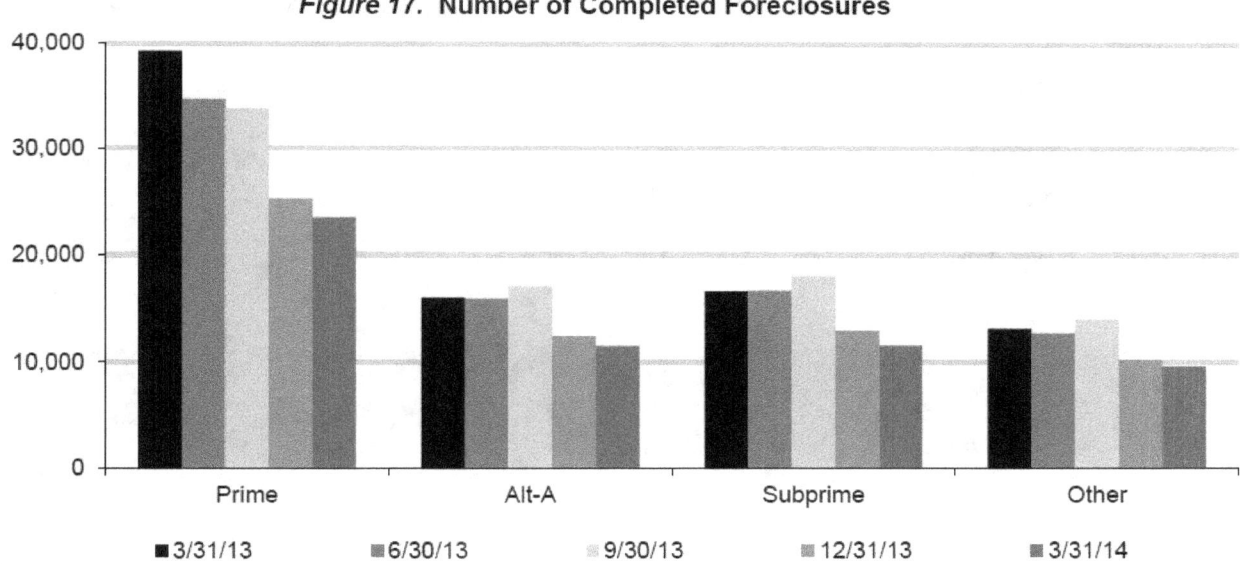

Figure 17. **Number of Completed Foreclosures**

Completed Short Sales and Deeds in Lieu of Foreclosure

The number of completed short sales and deeds in lieu of foreclosure decreased to 15,493 during the quarter—down 33.4 percent from the previous quarter and 66.9 percent from a year earlier. Short sales and deeds in lieu of foreclosure as a percentage of all mortgages serviced at the end of the first quarter of 2014 were 0.06 percent, down 32.3 percent from the previous quarter and 62.2 percent from a year earlier.

	3/31/13	6/30/13	9/30/13	12/31/13	3/31/14	1Q %Change	1Y %Change
Table 47. Completed Short Sales and Deeds in Lieu of Foreclosure Percentage of Completed Foreclosures Relative to Mortgages in That Risk Category							
Prime	0.1%	0.1%	0.1%	0.07%	0.05%	-34.1%	-65.5%
Alt-A	0.2%	0.2%	0.2%	0.2%	0.1%	-32.0%	-58.3%
Subprime	0.3%	0.3%	0.3%	0.2%	0.2%	-28.0%	-55.5%
Other	0.1%	0.2%	0.1%	0.1%	0.08%	-26.3%	-46.4%
Total	0.2%	0.2%	0.1%	0.09%	0.06%	-32.3%	-62.2%
Number of Completed Short Sales and Deeds in Lieu of Foreclosure							
Prime	28,731	25,236	19,959	13,781	8,980	-34.8%	-68.7%
Alt-A	7,418	6,699	5,382	3,844	2,564	-33.3%	-65.4%
Subprime	6,494	5,762	4,658	3,203	2,218	-30.8%	-65.8%
Other	4,096	4,089	3,374	2,438	1,731	-29.0%	-57.7%
Overall	46,739	41,786	33,373	23,266	15,493	-33.4%	-66.9%

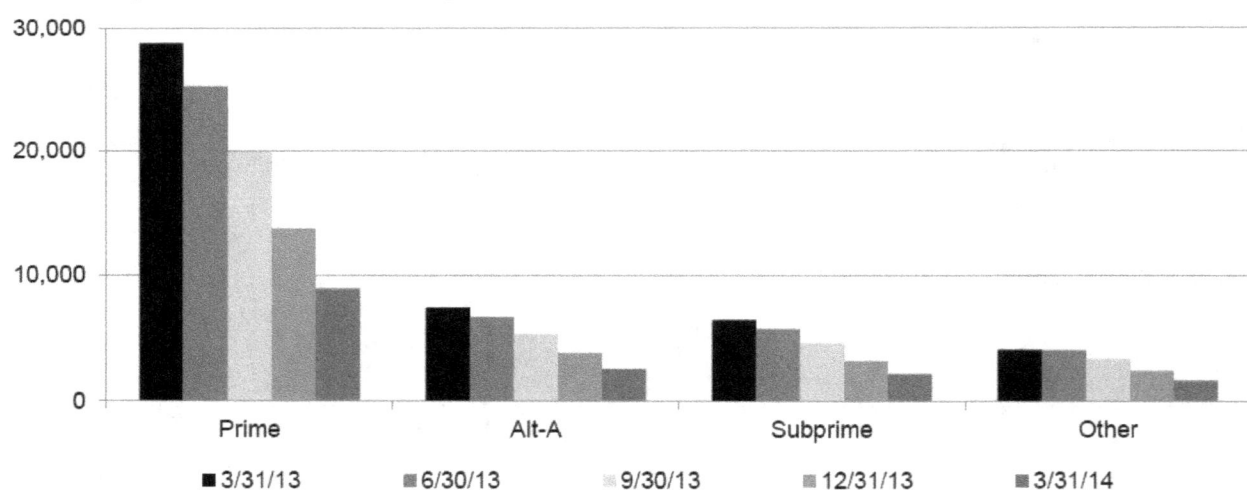

Figure 18. Number of Completed Short Sales and Deeds in Lieu of Foreclosure

New Home Retention Actions Relative to Forfeiture Actions, by Risk Category

New home retention actions continued to exceed completed home forfeitures as servicers initiated more than three times as many home retention actions as home forfeiture actions during the quarter. The percentage of new home retention actions relative to home forfeitures continued to be highest for Alt-A and subprime loans and lowest for prime and other loans during the first quarter of 2014.

Table 48. Percentage of New Home Retention Actions Relative to Forfeiture Actions, by Risk Category							
	3/31/13	6/30/13	9/30/13	12/31/13	3/31/14	1Q %Change	1Y %Change
Prime	229.3%	228.2%	239.5%	252.9%	292.0%	15.5%	27.3%
Alt-A	321.9%	313.3%	329.6%	359.9%	425.6%	18.2%	32.2%
Subprime	340.3%	309.8%	304.7%	328.4%	375.9%	14.4%	10.4%
Other	229.1%	232.3%	236.5%	258.8%	269.9%	4.3%	17.8%
Overall	265.2%	259.6%	269.2%	289.0%	330.8%	14.5%	24.7%

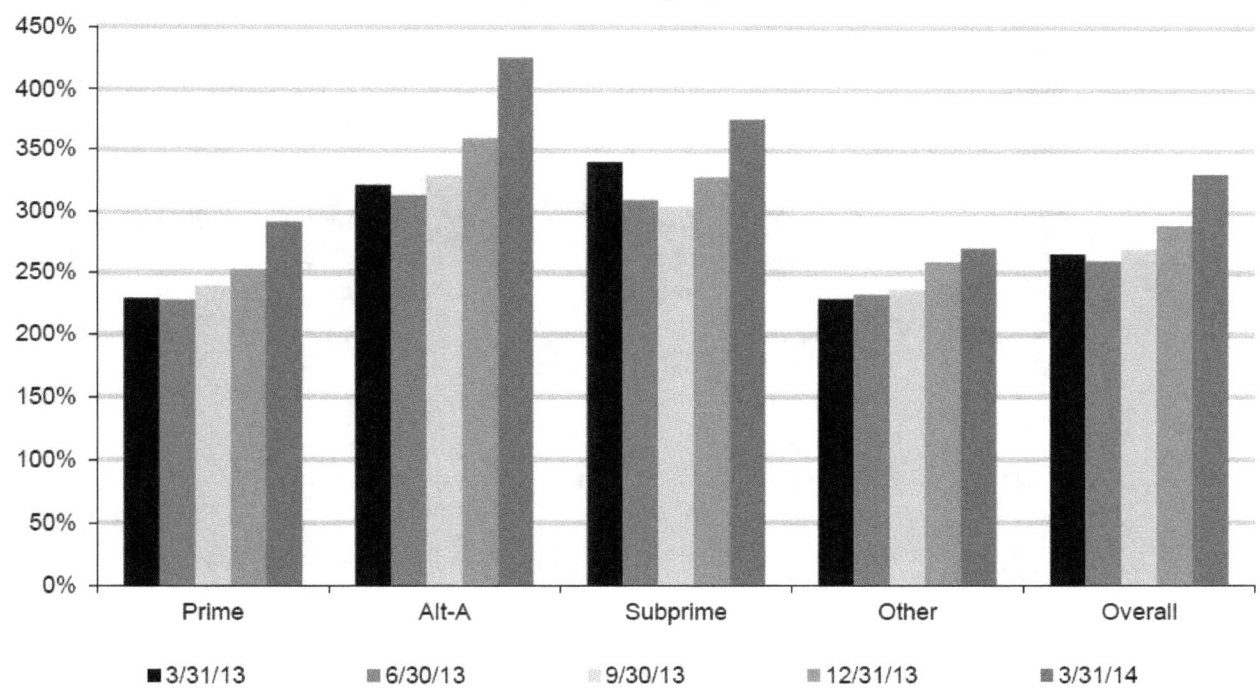

Figure 19. Percentage of New Home Retention Actions Relative to Forfeiture Actions, by Risk Category

Appendixes

Appendix A—New Loan Modifications

There were 65,437 loan modifications completed during the first quarter of 2014—a decrease of 9.7 percent from the previous quarter and 52.8 percent from a year earlier. Only modifications to Alt-A loans increased from the previous quarter.

Table 49. Number of New Loan Modifications							
	3/31/13	6/30/13	9/30/13	12/31/13	3/31/14	1Q %Change	1Y %Change
Prime	62,195	45,277	41,831	30,690	25,396	-17.2%	-59.2%
Alt-A	29,415	24,070	21,758	16,244	16,492	1.5%	-43.9%
Subprime	32,730	26,393	23,398	16,295	15,855	-2.7%	-51.6%
Other	14,209	12,455	12,306	9,237	7,694	-16.7%	-45.9%
Total	138,549	108,195	99,293	72,466	65,437	-9.7%	-52.8%

Figure 20. Number of New Loan Modifications

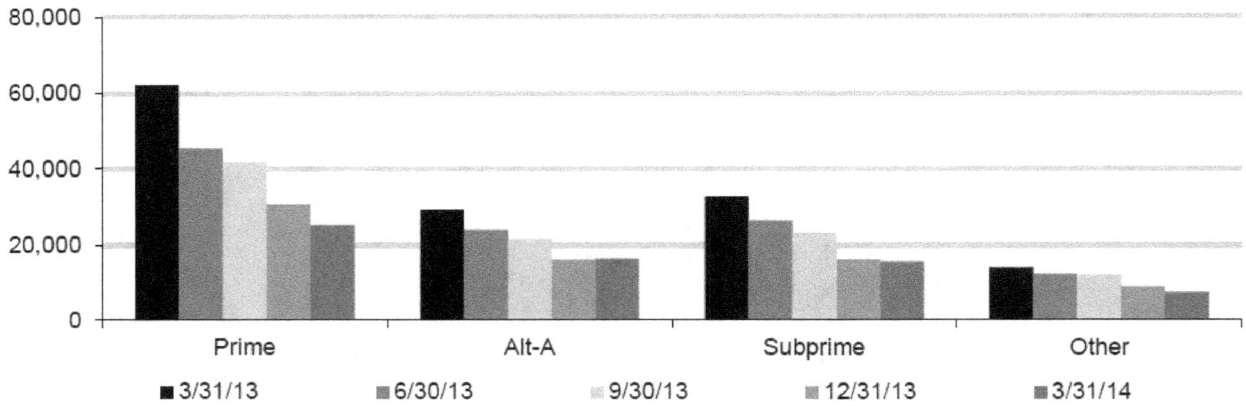

Appendix B—New Trial-Period Plans

Servicers initiated 71,381 trial-period plans during the first quarter of 2014, a decrease of 13.2 percent from the previous quarter and 31.1 percent from a year earlier.

	3/31/13	6/30/13	9/30/13	12/31/13	3/31/14	1Q %Change	1Y %Change
Prime	54,191	49,651	44,943	35,846	33,203	-7.4%	-38.7%
Alt-A	22,248	22,289	24,505	20,350	17,231	-15.3%	-22.6%
Subprime	19,413	19,021	21,178	17,499	14,552	-16.8%	-25.0%
Other	7,809	9,532	10,341	8,575	6,395	-25.4%	-18.1%
Total	103,661	100,493	100,967	82,270	71,381	-13.2%	-31.1%

Table 50. Number of New Trial-Period Plans

Figure 21. Number of New Trial-Period Plans

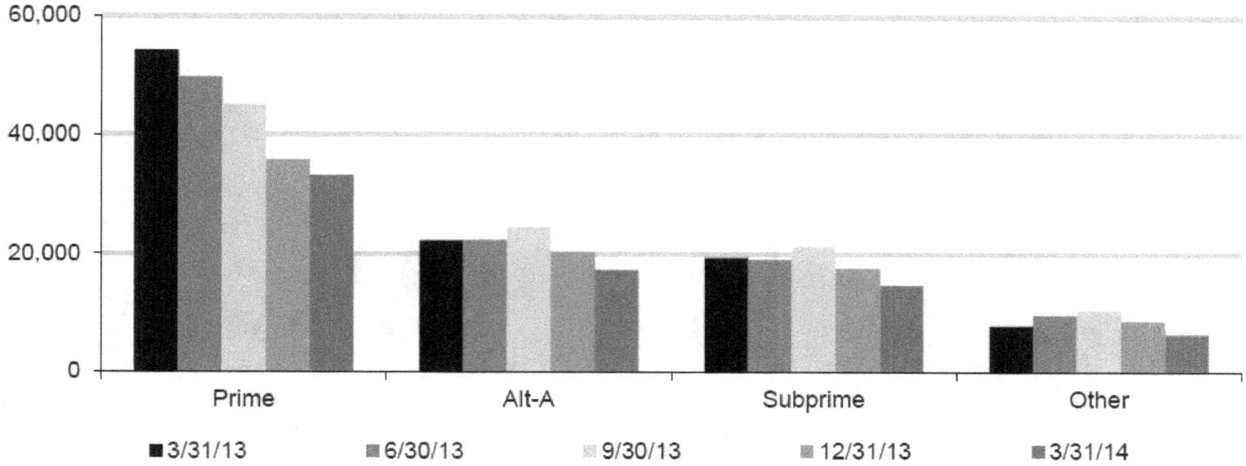

Appendix C—New Payment Plans

New payment plans increased by 13.9 percent during the first quarter of 2014 to 100,315, a decrease of 6.3 percent from a year earlier.

	3/31/13	6/30/13	9/30/13	12/31/13	3/31/14	1Q %Change	1Y %Change
Prime	39,529	41,831	42,039	32,195	36,392	13.0%	-7.9%
Alt-A	23,725	24,587	27,712	21,908	26,135	19.3%	10.2%
Subprime	26,409	24,023	24,448	19,100	21,300	11.5%	-19.3%
Other	17,450	16,962	18,369	14,890	16,488	10.7%	-5.5%
Total	107,113	107,403	112,568	88,093	100,315	13.9%	-6.3%

Table 51. Number of New Payment Plans

Figure 22. Number of New Payment Plans

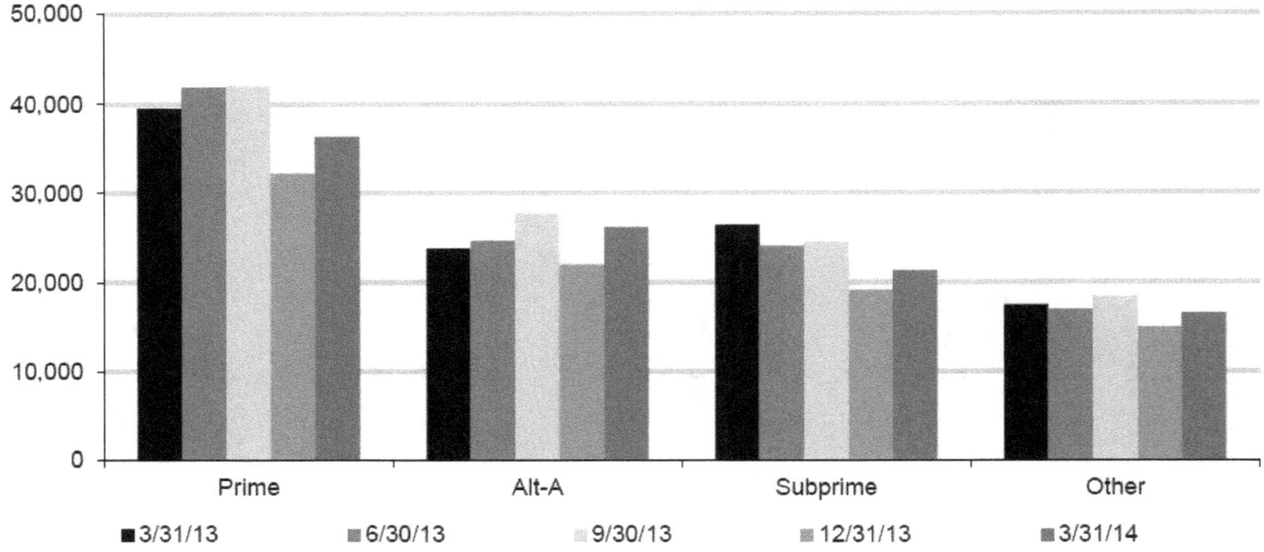

Appendix D—Breakdown of Individual and Combination Modification Actions

Servicers generally use a combination of actions to reduce monthly payments and achieve payment sustainability when modifying a mortgage. Servicers changed more than one loan term in 92.8 percent of all modifications completed during the first quarter of 2014.

Table 52. Changes in Terms for Modifications Made Through the First Quarter of 2014							
(Percentage of Modifications in Each Category)							
	3/31/13	6/30/13	9/30/13	12/31/13	3/31/14	1Q %Change	1Y %Change
Combination*	85.8%	89.7%	92.3%	95.5%	92.8%	-2.8%	8.2%
Capitalization	1.7%	1.8%	2.1%	2.4%	2.9%	20.7%	75.1%
Rate Reduction	11.1%	5.6%	2.5%	0.7%	0.3%	-59.7%	-97.5%
Rate Freeze	0.01%	0.00%	0.01%	0.01%	0.01%	32.9%	5.9%
Term Extension	0.6%	1.2%	0.6%	0.5%	3.1%	524.0%	393.3%
Principal Reduction	0.07%	0.08%	0.01%	0.01%	0.02%	60.0%	-73.3%
Principal Deferral	0.09%	0.1%	0.2%	0.2%	0.2%	0.8%	115.3%
Not Reported**	0.7%	1.5%	2.2%	0.7%	0.7%	-5.6%	-1.7%
(Number of Changes in Each Category)							
Combination	118,822	97,024	91,641	69,183	60,725	-12.2%	-48.9%
Capitalization	2,321	1,922	2,093	1,761	1,920	9.0%	-17.3%
Rate Reduction	15,365	6,113	2,471	505	184	-63.6%	-98.8%
Rate Freeze	12	3	6	5	6	20.0%	-50.0%
Term Extension	873	1,319	645	361	2,034	463.4%	133.0%
Principal Reduction	103	88	6	9	13	44.4%	-87.4%
Principal Deferral	120	155	240	134	122	-9.0%	1.7%
Not Reported	933	1,571	2,191	508	433	-14.8%	-53.6%
All Modifications	138,549	108,195	99,293	72,466	65,437	-9.7%	-52.8%

*Combination modifications result in a change to two or more loan terms. All other modification types detailed in this table involve only the individual listed action.

**See note to table 17.

Changes in Terms for Combination Modification Actions

Of the 60,725 modifications completed during the first quarter of 2014 that changed more than one term of the mortgage contract, 76.9 percent included capitalization of missed fees and payments, 78.6 percent included interest-rate reduction, and 80.7 percent included an extension of the loan maturity. Principal deferral was included in 26.9 percent of the combination modifications implemented during the quarter, and principal reduction was included in 8.7 percent. Because combination modifications changed more than one term, the sum of the individual actions exceeded 100 percent of total combination modifications.

Table 53. Changes in Terms for Combination Modifications Through the First Quarter of 2014
(Percentage of Modifications in Each Category)

	3/31/13	6/30/13	9/30/13	12/31/13	3/31/14	1Q %Change	1Y %Change
Capitalization	90.1%	89.0%	88.2%	89.3%	76.9%	-13.9%	-14.7%
Rate Reduction	80.4%	84.0%	82.8%	79.6%	78.6%	-1.2%	-2.2%
Rate Freeze	4.3%	5.8%	5.9%	7.3%	7.0%	-3.9%	63.7%
Term Extension	69.6%	74.1%	74.4%	79.0%	80.7%	2.1%	15.9%
Principal Reduction*	17.6%	13.5%	14.7%	11.0%	8.7%	-20.7%	-50.4%
Principal Deferral	21.2%	22.7%	27.2%	31.9%	26.9%	-15.7%	27.0%
(Number of Changes in Each Category)							
Capitalization	107,097	86,318	80,801	61,784	46,705	-24.4%	-56.4%
Rate Reduction	95,545	81,526	75,838	55,049	47,755	-13.3%	-50.0%
Rate Freeze	5,109	5,616	5,407	5,067	4,273	-15.7%	-16.4%
Term Extension	82,721	71,935	68,175	54,665	48,996	-10.4%	-40.8%
Principal Reduction	20,930	13,062	13,496	7,625	5,309	-30.4%	-74.6%
Principal Deferral	25,152	22,040	24,910	22,061	16,328	-26.0%	-35.1%

*See note to table 17.

Appendix E—Mortgage Modification Data by State

The following tables present certain mortgage modification data by state, the District of Columbia, and U.S. territories (the latter are included in the category labeled "Other"). These data fulfill reporting requirements in the Dodd–Frank Wall Street Reform and Consumer Protection Act of 2010 (Public Law 111-203).

Table 54 presents the number and percentage of HAMP modifications and other modifications in each state during the first quarter of 2014. Tables 55 and 56 present the number and percentage of each type of action included in modifications made during the quarter in each state, the District of Columbia, and U.S. territories. Tables 57 and 58 present the number and percentage of each type of action included in combination modifications made during the quarter in each state, the District of Columbia, and U.S. territories. Tables 59 and 60 present the number and percentage of modifications made during the quarter in each state, the District of Columbia, and U.S. territories by the amount of change in the borrowers' monthly principal and interest payments. Tables 61 and 62 present the number and percentage of modifications made in the third quarter of 2013 that were 60 or more days delinquent or in the process of foreclosure at the end of the first quarter of 2014.

Table 54. Number and Percentage of Mortgage Modifications Implemented in the First Quarter of 2014						
	HAMP Modifications		Other Modifications		Total Modifications	
States	Total	% of State Total	Total	% of State Total	Total	% of Total
Total - All States	31,030	47.4%	34,407	52.6%	65,437	100.0%
Alabama	373	45.7%	443	54.3%	816	1.2%
Alaska	30	60.0%	20	40.0%	50	0.1%
Arizona	517	47.4%	574	52.6%	1,091	1.7%
Arkansas	217	53.1%	192	46.9%	409	0.6%
California	3,012	40.7%	4,391	59.3%	7,403	11.3%
Colorado	439	52.4%	398	47.6%	837	1.3%
Connecticut	448	42.6%	604	57.4%	1,052	1.6%
Delaware	146	45.8%	173	54.2%	319	0.5%
District of Columbia	34	30.4%	78	69.6%	112	0.2%
Florida	2,806	43.5%	3,650	56.5%	6,456	9.9%
Georgia	1,595	50.7%	1,554	49.3%	3,149	4.8%
Hawaii	46	30.5%	105	69.5%	151	0.2%
Idaho	91	41.0%	131	59.0%	222	0.3%
Illinois	1,673	48.0%	1,809	52.0%	3,482	5.3%
Indiana	813	58.8%	569	41.2%	1,382	2.1%
Iowa	184	47.1%	207	52.9%	391	0.6%
Kansas	193	50.4%	190	49.6%	383	0.6%
Kentucky	251	47.1%	282	52.9%	533	0.8%
Louisiana	300	43.0%	398	57.0%	698	1.1%
Maine	90	39.3%	139	60.7%	229	0.3%
Maryland	1,108	46.2%	1,292	53.8%	2,400	3.7%
Massachusetts	520	41.4%	736	58.6%	1,256	1.9%
Michigan	643	44.8%	791	55.2%	1,434	2.2%
Minnesota	576	49.9%	579	50.1%	1,155	1.8%
Mississippi	144	42.9%	192	57.1%	336	0.5%
Missouri	605	51.4%	573	48.6%	1,178	1.8%
Montana	44	50.0%	44	50.0%	88	0.1%
Nebraska	127	50.2%	126	49.8%	253	0.4%
Nevada	370	41.8%	516	58.2%	886	1.4%
New Hampshire	90	38.0%	147	62.0%	237	0.4%
New Jersey	1,491	48.4%	1,592	51.6%	3,083	4.7%
New Mexico	171	49.1%	177	50.9%	348	0.5%
New York	2,052	48.1%	2,210	51.9%	4,262	6.5%
North Carolina	1,039	47.1%	1,168	52.9%	2,207	3.4%
North Dakota	7	46.7%	8	53.3%	15	0.0%
Ohio	1,193	53.9%	1,020	46.1%	2,213	3.4%
Oklahoma	223	52.5%	202	47.5%	425	0.6%
Oregon	257	40.9%	372	59.1%	629	1.0%
Pennsylvania	1,279	49.1%	1,327	50.9%	2,606	4.0%
Rhode Island	141	47.2%	158	52.8%	299	0.5%
South Carolina	417	45.4%	502	54.6%	919	1.4%
South Dakota	19	39.6%	29	60.4%	48	0.1%
Tennessee	589	51.7%	550	48.3%	1,139	1.7%
Texas	2,572	61.0%	1,645	39.0%	4,217	6.4%
Utah	278	54.4%	233	45.6%	511	0.8%
Vermont	25	29.8%	59	70.2%	84	0.1%
Virginia	719	46.8%	817	53.2%	1,536	2.3%
Washington	596	44.6%	741	55.4%	1,337	2.0%
West Virginia	59	34.3%	113	65.7%	172	0.3%
Wisconsin	359	44.1%	455	55.9%	814	1.2%
Wyoming	21	46.7%	24	53.3%	45	0.1%
Other	38	27.1%	102	72.9%	140	0.2%

States	Capitalization	Rate Reduction or Freeze	Term Extension	Principal Reductions	Principal Deferral	Combination	Not Reported	Total Modifications
Table 55. Number of Mortgage Modification Actions Implemented in the First Quarter of 2014								
Total - All States	1,920	190	2,034	13	122	60,725	433	65,437
Alabama	26	1	24	1	1	761	2	816
Alaska	2	-	3	-	-	45	-	50
Arizona	35	5	34	1	1	1,013	2	1,091
Arkansas	7	-	6	-	-	396	-	409
California	287	54	188	6	25	6,786	57	7,403
Colorado	24	3	50	-	-	759	1	837
Connecticut	29	4	23	-	1	987	8	1,052
Delaware	8	1	18	-	1	290	1	319
District of Columbia	9	-	-	-	-	102	1	112
Florida	138	30	70	1	11	6,178	28	6,456
Georgia	97	7	119	-	7	2,899	20	3,149
Hawaii	6	-	4	-	-	141	-	151
Idaho	4	1	3	-	-	214	-	222
Illinois	65	4	117	1	3	3,278	14	3,482
Indiana	29	2	38	-	-	1,309	4	1,382
Iowa	10	-	12	-	-	369	-	391
Kansas	17	-	8	-	-	358	-	383
Kentucky	16	2	9	-	-	505	1	533
Louisiana	20	1	23	-	-	653	1	698
Maine	7	1	9	-	-	209	3	229
Maryland	76	11	123	-	17	2,157	16	2,400
Massachusetts	66	5	34	-	4	1,133	14	1,256
Michigan	47	-	32	-	-	1,350	5	1,434
Minnesota	20	1	44	-	1	1,085	4	1,155
Mississippi	19	2	8	-	-	306	1	336
Missouri	45	-	29	-	2	1,098	4	1,178
Montana	3	1	2	-	-	82	-	88
Nebraska	8	-	5	-	-	240	-	253
Nevada	30	6	26	1	4	816	3	886
New Hampshire	7	1	7	-	-	221	1	237
New Jersey	52	4	94	2	10	2,899	22	3,083
New Mexico	17	-	8	-	-	323	-	348
New York	71	16	78	-	16	3,936	145	4,262
North Carolina	92	1	105	-	3	1,989	17	2,207
North Dakota	1	-	-	-	-	14	-	15
Ohio	45	6	69	-	1	2,085	7	2,213
Oklahoma	18	-	9	-	-	397	1	425
Oregon	22	2	19	-	1	585	-	629
Pennsylvania	77	2	91	-	5	2,408	23	2,606
Rhode Island	8	-	14	-	-	276	1	299
South Carolina	33	1	25	-	1	858	1	919
South Dakota	4	-	1	-	1	42	-	48
Tennessee	40	1	36	-	-	1,062	-	1,139
Texas	140	5	219	-	-	3,842	11	4,217
Utah	12	1	40	-	1	457	-	511
Vermont	3	-	-	-	-	79	2	84
Virginia	53	1	70	-	1	1,403	8	1,536
Washington	38	4	63	-	4	1,226	2	1,337
West Virginia	11	-	4	-	-	156	1	172
Wisconsin	22	3	21	-	-	768	-	814
Wyoming	1	-	-	-	-	43	1	45
Other	3	-	-	-	-	137	-	140

Table 56. Percentage of Mortgage Modification Actions Implemented in the First Quarter of 2014							
States	Capitalization	Rate Reduction or Freeze	Term Extension	Principal Reduction	Principal Deferral	Combination	Not Reported	Total Modifications
Total - All States	2.9%	0.3%	3.1%	0.0%	0.2%	92.8%	0.7%	65,437
Alabama	3.2%	0.1%	2.9%	0.1%	0.1%	93.3%	0.2%	816
Alaska	4.0%	0.0%	6.0%	0.0%	0.0%	90.0%	0.0%	50
Arizona	3.2%	0.5%	3.1%	0.1%	0.1%	92.9%	0.2%	1,091
Arkansas	1.7%	0.0%	1.5%	0.0%	0.0%	96.8%	0.0%	409
California	3.9%	0.7%	2.5%	0.1%	0.3%	91.7%	0.8%	7,403
Colorado	2.9%	0.4%	6.0%	0.0%	0.0%	90.7%	0.1%	837
Connecticut	2.8%	0.4%	2.2%	0.0%	0.1%	93.8%	0.8%	1,052
Delaware	2.5%	0.3%	5.6%	0.0%	0.3%	90.9%	0.3%	319
District of Columbia	8.0%	0.0%	0.0%	0.0%	0.0%	91.1%	0.9%	112
Florida	2.1%	0.5%	1.1%	0.0%	0.2%	95.7%	0.4%	6,456
Georgia	3.1%	0.2%	3.8%	0.0%	0.2%	92.1%	0.6%	3,149
Hawaii	4.0%	0.0%	2.6%	0.0%	0.0%	93.4%	0.0%	151
Idaho	1.8%	0.5%	1.4%	0.0%	0.0%	96.4%	0.0%	222
Illinois	1.9%	0.1%	3.4%	0.0%	0.1%	94.1%	0.4%	3,482
Indiana	2.1%	0.1%	2.7%	0.0%	0.0%	94.7%	0.3%	1,382
Iowa	2.6%	0.0%	3.1%	0.0%	0.0%	94.4%	0.0%	391
Kansas	4.4%	0.0%	2.1%	0.0%	0.0%	93.5%	0.0%	383
Kentucky	3.0%	0.4%	1.7%	0.0%	0.0%	94.7%	0.2%	533
Louisiana	2.9%	0.1%	3.3%	0.0%	0.0%	93.6%	0.1%	698
Maine	3.1%	0.4%	3.9%	0.0%	0.0%	91.3%	1.3%	229
Maryland	3.2%	0.5%	5.1%	0.0%	0.7%	89.9%	0.7%	2,400
Massachusetts	5.3%	0.4%	2.7%	0.0%	0.3%	90.2%	1.1%	1,256
Michigan	3.3%	0.0%	2.2%	0.0%	0.0%	94.1%	0.3%	1,434
Minnesota	1.7%	0.1%	3.8%	0.0%	0.1%	93.9%	0.3%	1,155
Mississippi	5.7%	0.6%	2.4%	0.0%	0.0%	91.1%	0.3%	336
Missouri	3.8%	0.0%	2.5%	0.0%	0.2%	93.2%	0.3%	1,178
Montana	3.4%	1.1%	2.3%	0.0%	0.0%	93.2%	0.0%	88
Nebraska	3.2%	0.0%	2.0%	0.0%	0.0%	94.9%	0.0%	253
Nevada	3.4%	0.7%	2.9%	0.1%	0.5%	92.1%	0.3%	886
New Hampshire	3.0%	0.4%	3.0%	0.0%	0.0%	93.2%	0.4%	237
New Jersey	1.7%	0.1%	3.0%	0.1%	0.3%	94.0%	0.7%	3,083
New Mexico	4.9%	0.0%	2.3%	0.0%	0.0%	92.8%	0.0%	348
New York	1.7%	0.4%	1.8%	0.0%	0.4%	92.4%	3.4%	4,262
North Carolina	4.2%	0.0%	4.8%	0.0%	0.1%	90.1%	0.8%	2,207
North Dakota	6.7%	0.0%	0.0%	0.0%	0.0%	93.3%	0.0%	15
Ohio	2.0%	0.3%	3.1%	0.0%	0.0%	94.2%	0.3%	2,213
Oklahoma	4.2%	0.0%	2.1%	0.0%	0.0%	93.4%	0.2%	425
Oregon	3.5%	0.3%	3.0%	0.0%	0.2%	93.0%	0.0%	629
Pennsylvania	3.0%	0.1%	3.5%	0.0%	0.2%	92.4%	0.9%	2,606
Rhode Island	2.7%	0.0%	4.7%	0.0%	0.0%	92.3%	0.3%	299
South Carolina	3.6%	0.1%	2.7%	0.0%	0.1%	93.4%	0.1%	919
South Dakota	8.3%	0.0%	2.1%	0.0%	2.1%	87.5%	0.0%	48
Tennessee	3.5%	0.1%	3.2%	0.0%	0.0%	93.2%	0.0%	1,139
Texas	3.3%	0.1%	5.2%	0.0%	0.0%	91.1%	0.3%	4,217
Utah	2.3%	0.2%	7.8%	0.0%	0.2%	89.4%	0.0%	511
Vermont	3.6%	0.0%	0.0%	0.0%	0.0%	94.0%	2.4%	84
Virginia	3.5%	0.1%	4.6%	0.0%	0.1%	91.3%	0.5%	1,536
Washington	2.8%	0.3%	4.7%	0.0%	0.3%	91.7%	0.1%	1,337
West Virginia	6.4%	0.0%	2.3%	0.0%	0.0%	90.7%	0.6%	172
Wisconsin	2.7%	0.4%	2.6%	0.0%	0.0%	94.3%	0.0%	814
Wyoming	2.2%	0.0%	0.0%	0.0%	0.0%	95.6%	2.2%	45
Other	2.1%	0.0%	0.0%	0.0%	0.0%	97.9%	0.0%	140

	Table 57. Number of Modification Actions in Combination Actions Implemented in the First Quarter of 2014					
States	Capitalization	Rate Reduction or Freeze	Term Extension	Principal Reduction	Principal Deferral	Total Combination Modifications
Total - All States	46,705	51,779	48,996	5,309	16,328	60,725
Alabama	574	659	658	20	132	761
Alaska	26	39	41	2	3	45
Arizona	750	853	784	103	291	1,013
Arkansas	271	356	327	5	79	396
California	5,851	5,493	4,578	1,358	2,020	6,786
Colorado	515	648	641	22	119	759
Connecticut	820	826	766	127	307	987
Delaware	233	236	246	23	77	290
District of Columbia	95	78	76	5	24	102
Florida	5,298	5,188	4,724	958	2,338	6,178
Georgia	2,103	2,541	2,362	200	858	2,899
Hawaii	133	115	90	8	32	141
Idaho	160	179	184	8	43	214
Illinois	2,543	2,800	2,703	340	1,186	3,278
Indiana	837	1,167	1,150	34	282	1,309
Iowa	248	304	313	10	46	369
Kansas	215	308	321	6	58	358
Kentucky	386	441	434	16	77	505
Louisiana	501	569	516	17	105	653
Maine	168	173	159	10	46	209
Maryland	1,710	1,787	1,683	228	669	2,157
Massachusetts	930	908	902	87	289	1,133
Michigan	1,063	1,179	1,093	99	398	1,350
Minnesota	762	952	938	42	235	1,085
Mississippi	235	267	244	23	61	306
Missouri	772	965	920	79	250	1,098
Montana	57	62	72	1	16	82
Nebraska	143	212	212	3	27	240
Nevada	626	655	625	96	312	816
New Hampshire	176	178	175	16	54	221
New Jersey	2,298	2,431	2,411	264	873	2,899
New Mexico	221	287	268	23	57	323
New York	3,281	3,352	3,277	225	1,231	3,936
North Carolina	1,473	1,707	1,673	82	385	1,989
North Dakota	9	12	12	-	2	14
Ohio	1,420	1,867	1,821	101	453	2,085
Oklahoma	257	358	338	5	59	397
Oregon	469	497	474	40	112	585
Pennsylvania	1,790	2,052	2,018	123	531	2,408
Rhode Island	206	233	213	37	88	276
South Carolina	640	728	724	41	169	858
South Dakota	31	33	38	-	4	42
Tennessee	757	954	880	47	218	1,062
Texas	2,364	3,493	3,359	108	768	3,842
Utah	297	396	397	15	77	457
Vermont	63	65	61	4	15	79
Virginia	1,089	1,200	1,126	87	323	1,403
Washington	930	1,028	1,019	99	294	1,226
West Virginia	128	128	136	7	23	156
Wisconsin	619	654	658	49	203	768
Wyoming	33	40	35	4	5	43
Other	129	126	121	2	4	137

Table 58. Percentage of Modification Actions in Combination Actions Implemented in the First Quarter of 2014						
States	Capitalization	Rate Reduction or Freeze	Term Extension	Principal Reduction	Principal Deferral	Total Combination Modifications
Total - All States	76.9%	85.3%	80.7%	8.7%	26.9%	60,725
Alabama	75.4%	86.6%	86.5%	2.6%	17.3%	761
Alaska	57.8%	86.7%	91.1%	4.4%	6.7%	45
Arizona	74.0%	84.2%	77.4%	10.2%	28.7%	1,013
Arkansas	68.4%	89.9%	82.6%	1.3%	19.9%	396
California	86.2%	80.9%	67.5%	20.0%	29.8%	6,786
Colorado	67.9%	85.4%	84.5%	2.9%	15.7%	759
Connecticut	83.1%	83.7%	77.6%	12.9%	31.1%	987
Delaware	80.3%	81.4%	84.8%	7.9%	26.6%	290
District of Columbia	93.1%	76.5%	74.5%	4.9%	23.5%	102
Florida	85.8%	84.0%	76.5%	15.5%	37.8%	6,178
Georgia	72.5%	87.7%	81.5%	6.9%	29.6%	2,899
Hawaii	94.3%	81.6%	63.8%	5.7%	22.7%	141
Idaho	74.8%	83.6%	86.0%	3.7%	20.1%	214
Illinois	77.6%	85.4%	82.5%	10.4%	36.2%	3,278
Indiana	63.9%	89.2%	87.9%	2.6%	21.5%	1,309
Iowa	67.2%	82.4%	84.8%	2.7%	12.5%	369
Kansas	60.1%	86.0%	89.7%	1.7%	16.2%	358
Kentucky	76.4%	87.3%	85.9%	3.2%	15.2%	505
Louisiana	76.7%	87.1%	79.0%	2.6%	16.1%	653
Maine	80.4%	82.8%	76.1%	4.8%	22.0%	209
Maryland	79.3%	82.8%	78.0%	10.6%	31.0%	2,157
Massachusetts	82.1%	80.1%	79.6%	7.7%	25.5%	1,133
Michigan	78.7%	87.3%	81.0%	7.3%	29.5%	1,350
Minnesota	70.2%	87.7%	86.5%	3.9%	21.7%	1,085
Mississippi	76.8%	87.3%	79.7%	7.5%	19.9%	306
Missouri	70.3%	87.9%	83.8%	7.2%	22.8%	1,098
Montana	69.5%	75.6%	87.8%	1.2%	19.5%	82
Nebraska	59.6%	88.3%	88.3%	1.3%	11.3%	240
Nevada	76.7%	80.3%	76.6%	11.8%	38.2%	816
New Hampshire	79.6%	80.5%	79.2%	7.2%	24.4%	221
New Jersey	79.3%	83.9%	83.2%	9.1%	30.1%	2,899
New Mexico	68.4%	88.9%	83.0%	7.1%	17.6%	323
New York	83.4%	85.2%	83.3%	5.7%	31.3%	3,936
North Carolina	74.1%	85.8%	84.1%	4.1%	19.4%	1,989
North Dakota	64.3%	85.7%	85.7%	0.0%	14.3%	14
Ohio	68.1%	89.5%	87.3%	4.8%	21.7%	2,085
Oklahoma	64.7%	90.2%	85.1%	1.3%	14.9%	397
Oregon	80.2%	85.0%	81.0%	6.8%	19.1%	585
Pennsylvania	74.3%	85.2%	83.8%	5.1%	22.1%	2,408
Rhode Island	74.6%	84.4%	77.2%	13.4%	31.9%	276
South Carolina	74.6%	84.8%	84.4%	4.8%	19.7%	858
South Dakota	73.8%	78.6%	90.5%	0.0%	9.5%	42
Tennessee	71.3%	89.8%	82.9%	4.4%	20.5%	1,062
Texas	61.5%	90.9%	87.4%	2.8%	20.0%	3,842
Utah	65.0%	86.7%	86.9%	3.3%	16.8%	457
Vermont	79.7%	82.3%	77.2%	5.1%	19.0%	79
Virginia	77.6%	85.5%	80.3%	6.2%	23.0%	1,403
Washington	75.9%	83.8%	83.1%	8.1%	24.0%	1,226
West Virginia	82.1%	82.1%	87.2%	4.5%	14.7%	156
Wisconsin	80.6%	85.2%	85.7%	6.4%	26.4%	768
Wyoming	76.7%	93.0%	81.4%	9.3%	11.6%	43
Other	94.2%	92.0%	88.3%	1.5%	2.9%	137

		Table 59. Changes in Monthly Principal and Interest Payments by State (Number) Modifications Implemented in the First Quarter of 2014					
States	Decreased by 20% or More	Decreased by 10% to Less Than 20%	Decreased by Less Than 10%	Unchanged	Increased	Not Reported	Total Modifications
Total - All States	38,026	13,266	7,623	1,145	4,796	581	65,437
Alabama	434	186	97	14	61	24	816
Alaska	26	11	6	-	7	-	50
Arizona	615	237	148	21	67	3	1,091
Arkansas	234	73	58	9	34	1	409
California	4,362	1,402	868	98	617	56	7,403
Colorado	437	206	111	11	67	5	837
Connecticut	643	213	91	14	87	4	1,052
Delaware	156	85	45	8	25	-	319
District of Columbia	58	21	11	1	20	1	112
Florida	4,170	1,046	618	95	483	44	6,456
Georgia	1,900	608	344	72	191	34	3,149
Hawaii	83	37	15	3	11	2	151
Idaho	118	55	25	4	16	4	222
Illinois	2,228	649	350	52	188	15	3,482
Indiana	734	339	166	41	86	16	1,382
Iowa	187	103	58	10	31	2	391
Kansas	199	94	41	10	35	4	383
Kentucky	271	125	82	12	38	5	533
Louisiana	357	136	101	18	65	21	698
Maine	132	38	31	5	21	2	229
Maryland	1,308	519	331	38	185	19	2,400
Massachusetts	734	247	154	12	100	9	1,256
Michigan	890	270	143	36	82	13	1,434
Minnesota	675	253	139	19	65	4	1,155
Mississippi	170	75	45	7	38	1	336
Missouri	664	257	159	12	78	8	1,178
Montana	37	24	10	2	13	2	88
Nebraska	122	54	42	6	25	4	253
Nevada	539	171	104	15	55	2	886
New Hampshire	128	51	34	1	21	2	237
New Jersey	1,868	637	312	42	198	26	3,083
New Mexico	189	70	51	6	30	2	348
New York	2,659	759	410	44	277	113	4,262
North Carolina	1,153	517	294	46	167	30	2,207
North Dakota	5	3	3	1	3	-	15
Ohio	1,293	469	250	56	132	13	2,213
Oklahoma	228	87	57	10	41	2	425
Oregon	343	136	90	6	51	3	629
Pennsylvania	1,487	536	305	49	207	22	2,606
Rhode Island	193	57	29	4	15	1	299
South Carolina	478	207	122	24	81	7	919
South Dakota	24	8	8	1	7	-	48
Tennessee	641	253	120	33	85	7	1,139
Texas	2,324	909	569	93	300	22	4,217
Utah	275	124	71	10	29	2	511
Vermont	48	15	7	2	10	2	84
Virginia	813	355	192	25	140	11	1,536
Washington	712	309	169	18	127	2	1,337
West Virginia	93	29	22	6	16	6	172
Wisconsin	463	173	101	18	57	2	814
Wyoming	21	11	8	1	3	1	45
Other	105	17	6	4	8	-	140

	Table 60. Changes in Monthly Principal and Interest Payments (Percentage)						
	Modifications Implemented in the First Quarter of 2014						
States	Decreased by 20% or More	Decreased by 10% to Less Than 20%	Decreased by Less Than 10%	Unchanged	Increased	Not Reported	Total Modifications
Total - All States	58.1%	20.3%	11.6%	1.7%	7.3%	0.9%	65,437
Alabama	53.2%	22.8%	11.9%	1.7%	7.5%	2.9%	816
Alaska	52.0%	22.0%	12.0%	0.0%	14.0%	0.0%	50
Arizona	56.4%	21.7%	13.6%	1.9%	6.1%	0.3%	1,091
Arkansas	57.2%	17.8%	14.2%	2.2%	8.3%	0.2%	409
California	58.9%	18.9%	11.7%	1.3%	8.3%	0.8%	7,403
Colorado	52.2%	24.6%	13.3%	1.3%	8.0%	0.6%	837
Connecticut	61.1%	20.2%	8.7%	1.3%	8.3%	0.4%	1,052
Delaware	48.9%	26.6%	14.1%	2.5%	7.8%	0.0%	319
District of Columbia	51.8%	18.8%	9.8%	0.9%	17.9%	0.9%	112
Florida	64.6%	16.2%	9.6%	1.5%	7.5%	0.7%	6,456
Georgia	60.3%	19.3%	10.9%	2.3%	6.1%	1.1%	3,149
Hawaii	55.0%	24.5%	9.9%	2.0%	7.3%	1.3%	151
Idaho	53.2%	24.8%	11.3%	1.8%	7.2%	1.8%	222
Illinois	64.0%	18.6%	10.1%	1.5%	5.4%	0.4%	3,482
Indiana	53.1%	24.5%	12.0%	3.0%	6.2%	1.2%	1,382
Iowa	47.8%	26.3%	14.8%	2.6%	7.9%	0.5%	391
Kansas	52.0%	24.5%	10.7%	2.6%	9.1%	1.0%	383
Kentucky	50.8%	23.5%	15.4%	2.3%	7.1%	0.9%	533
Louisiana	51.1%	19.5%	14.5%	2.6%	9.3%	3.0%	698
Maine	57.6%	16.6%	13.5%	2.2%	9.2%	0.9%	229
Maryland	54.5%	21.6%	13.8%	1.6%	7.7%	0.8%	2,400
Massachusetts	58.4%	19.7%	12.3%	1.0%	8.0%	0.7%	1,256
Michigan	62.1%	18.8%	10.0%	2.5%	5.7%	0.9%	1,434
Minnesota	58.4%	21.9%	12.0%	1.6%	5.6%	0.3%	1,155
Mississippi	50.6%	22.3%	13.4%	2.1%	11.3%	0.3%	336
Missouri	56.4%	21.8%	13.5%	1.0%	6.6%	0.7%	1,178
Montana	42.0%	27.3%	11.4%	2.3%	14.8%	2.3%	88
Nebraska	48.2%	21.3%	16.6%	2.4%	9.9%	1.6%	253
Nevada	60.8%	19.3%	11.7%	1.7%	6.2%	0.2%	886
New Hampshire	54.0%	21.5%	14.3%	0.4%	8.9%	0.8%	237
New Jersey	60.6%	20.7%	10.1%	1.4%	6.4%	0.8%	3,083
New Mexico	54.3%	20.1%	14.7%	1.7%	8.6%	0.6%	348
New York	62.4%	17.8%	9.6%	1.0%	6.5%	2.7%	4,262
North Carolina	52.2%	23.4%	13.3%	2.1%	7.6%	1.4%	2,207
North Dakota	33.3%	20.0%	20.0%	6.7%	20.0%	0.0%	15
Ohio	58.4%	21.2%	11.3%	2.5%	6.0%	0.6%	2,213
Oklahoma	53.6%	20.5%	13.4%	2.4%	9.6%	0.5%	425
Oregon	54.5%	21.6%	14.3%	1.0%	8.1%	0.5%	629
Pennsylvania	57.1%	20.6%	11.7%	1.9%	7.9%	0.8%	2,606
Rhode Island	64.5%	19.1%	9.7%	1.3%	5.0%	0.3%	299
South Carolina	52.0%	22.5%	13.3%	2.6%	8.8%	0.8%	919
South Dakota	50.0%	16.7%	16.7%	2.1%	14.6%	0.0%	48
Tennessee	56.3%	22.2%	10.5%	2.9%	7.5%	0.6%	1,139
Texas	55.1%	21.6%	13.5%	2.2%	7.1%	0.5%	4,217
Utah	53.8%	24.3%	13.9%	2.0%	5.7%	0.4%	511
Vermont	57.1%	17.9%	8.3%	2.4%	11.9%	2.4%	84
Virginia	52.9%	23.1%	12.5%	1.6%	9.1%	0.7%	1,536
Washington	53.3%	23.1%	12.6%	1.3%	9.5%	0.1%	1,337
West Virginia	54.1%	16.9%	12.8%	3.5%	9.3%	3.5%	172
Wisconsin	56.9%	21.3%	12.4%	2.2%	7.0%	0.2%	814
Wyoming	46.7%	24.4%	17.8%	2.2%	6.7%	2.2%	45
Other	75.0%	12.1%	4.3%	2.9%	5.7%	0.0%	140

Table 61. Number of Re-Defaults for Loans Modified in the Third Quarter of 2013
(60 or More Days Delinquent After 6 Months by Changes in Monthly Principal and Interest Payments)

States	Decreased by 20% or More	Decreased by 10% to Less Than 20%	Decreased by Less Than 10%	Unchanged	Increased	Not Reported	Total Modifications
Total - All States	5,369	2,828	2,245	121	1,379	120	12,062
Alabama	80	43	38	2	17	2	182
Alaska	2	-	1	-	3	-	6
Arizona	83	55	34	4	20	1	197
Arkansas	38	29	12	-	15	-	94
California	531	225	189	9	139	3	1,096
Colorado	43	41	31	1	11	1	128
Connecticut	79	41	33	1	13	5	172
Delaware	44	25	23	2	9	1	104
District of Columbia	7	10	6	-	3	-	26
Florida	438	188	129	7	105	11	878
Georgia	303	190	148	12	82	-	735
Hawaii	6	3	4	-	3	-	16
Idaho	19	9	8	-	8	-	44
Illinois	327	128	102	2	87	6	652
Indiana	90	74	45	-	23	7	239
Iowa	27	21	17	-	4	1	70
Kansas	35	18	13	-	9	-	75
Kentucky	45	27	19	2	14	1	108
Louisiana	61	46	41	2	26	3	179
Maine	20	11	13	-	4	-	48
Maryland	201	136	110	7	71	5	530
Massachusetts	127	68	30	2	18	2	247
Michigan	143	55	34	4	27	4	267
Minnesota	69	34	35	1	16	3	158
Mississippi	43	30	16	1	14	-	104
Missouri	93	42	35	1	18	-	189
Montana	6	3	-	-	1	-	10
Nebraska	7	5	6	-	5	2	25
Nevada	63	35	25	-	8	2	133
New Hampshire	20	8	7	-	4	-	39
New Jersey	286	122	124	8	65	2	607
New Mexico	40	13	6	-	6	1	66
New York	318	144	135	9	62	19	687
North Carolina	213	150	124	3	79	2	571
North Dakota	-	-	-	-	2	-	2
Ohio	168	96	75	3	39	16	397
Oklahoma	38	19	24	-	12	-	93
Oregon	48	32	8	-	5	-	93
Pennsylvania	250	104	99	5	61	5	524
Rhode Island	29	8	3	1	6	-	47
South Carolina	91	46	61	2	35	3	238
South Dakota	3	3	1	1	-	-	8
Tennessee	121	62	48	3	19	3	256
Texas	343	214	164	12	100	3	836
Utah	36	26	25	1	8	1	97
Vermont	7	1	1	-	1	-	10
Virginia	147	73	62	7	39	3	331
Washington	110	63	39	2	34	1	249
West Virginia	15	3	7	1	3	-	29
Wisconsin	52	48	30	1	26	1	158
Wyoming	1	1	2	-	-	-	4
Other	3	-	3	2	-	-	8

Table 62. Re-Default Rates for Loans Modified in the Third Quarter of 2013 (Percentage)
(60 or More Days Delinquent After 6 Months by Changes in Monthly Principal and Interest Payments)

States	Decreased by 20% or More	Decreased by 10% to Less Than 20%	Decreased by Less Than 10%	Unchanged	Increased	Not Reported	Total Modifications
Total - All States	9.9%	17.1%	22.9%	21.3%	23.3%	21.0%	13.8%
Alabama	14.8%	20.4%	30.2%	18.2%	25.4%	50.0%	19.0%
Alaska	9.5%	0.0%	12.5%	0.0%	60.0%	0.0%	15.4%
Arizona	8.6%	15.9%	19.4%	33.3%	18.0%	16.7%	12.2%
Arkansas	17.5%	25.7%	24.5%	0.0%	30.6%	0.0%	21.4%
California	5.8%	10.0%	13.7%	8.4%	13.0%	8.6%	7.8%
Colorado	7.2%	13.9%	17.3%	20.0%	15.3%	20.0%	11.1%
Connecticut	9.5%	19.0%	24.3%	16.7%	15.5%	50.0%	13.4%
Delaware	15.4%	25.0%	34.8%	66.7%	28.1%	100.0%	21.3%
District of Columbia	8.9%	19.2%	18.8%	0.0%	21.4%	0.0%	14.6%
Florida	7.1%	13.5%	15.7%	13.5%	19.0%	13.8%	9.7%
Georgia	11.1%	20.7%	29.8%	29.3%	31.7%	0.0%	16.5%
Hawaii	5.0%	10.3%	17.4%	0.0%	18.8%	0.0%	8.5%
Idaho	9.5%	12.2%	19.5%	0.0%	30.8%	0.0%	12.8%
Illinois	9.7%	16.5%	22.5%	11.8%	29.9%	24.0%	13.3%
Indiana	10.4%	23.9%	25.0%	0.0%	23.2%	24.1%	16.0%
Iowa	12.3%	26.6%	28.3%	0.0%	11.4%	33.3%	17.5%
Kansas	16.2%	22.2%	24.1%	0.0%	26.5%	0.0%	18.9%
Kentucky	13.8%	17.9%	21.3%	33.3%	31.1%	20.0%	17.3%
Louisiana	12.5%	21.2%	29.9%	33.3%	28.6%	15.8%	18.7%
Maine	13.2%	18.0%	31.7%	0.0%	19.0%	0.0%	17.5%
Maryland	11.4%	20.4%	24.6%	31.8%	30.2%	50.0%	16.9%
Massachusetts	12.4%	22.2%	17.4%	18.2%	20.2%	13.3%	15.3%
Michigan	10.5%	15.7%	20.4%	36.4%	24.5%	19.0%	13.2%
Minnesota	10.2%	15.1%	29.7%	14.3%	22.2%	7.3%	13.8%
Mississippi	14.2%	28.0%	26.2%	11.1%	28.0%	0.0%	19.4%
Missouri	12.8%	15.6%	25.2%	16.7%	26.5%	0.0%	15.5%
Montana	10.0%	10.0%	0.0%	0.0%	7.7%	0.0%	8.1%
Nebraska	6.5%	11.4%	27.3%	0.0%	41.7%	20.0%	12.8%
Nevada	7.3%	15.7%	21.0%	0.0%	12.9%	25.0%	10.4%
New Hampshire	9.6%	12.3%	19.4%	0.0%	19.0%	0.0%	11.8%
New Jersey	11.7%	17.7%	28.4%	34.8%	29.4%	20.0%	15.9%
New Mexico	13.6%	15.3%	11.8%	0.0%	24.0%	33.3%	14.3%
New York	9.7%	15.2%	25.9%	33.3%	24.4%	54.3%	13.6%
North Carolina	12.8%	22.6%	31.0%	16.7%	33.2%	20.0%	19.1%
North Dakota	0.0%	0.0%	0.0%	0.0%	100.0%	0.0%	10.0%
Ohio	10.9%	19.4%	25.0%	21.4%	23.9%	28.6%	15.4%
Oklahoma	13.6%	15.3%	31.6%	0.0%	26.7%	0.0%	17.3%
Oregon	8.1%	16.6%	7.8%	0.0%	10.4%	0.0%	9.9%
Pennsylvania	14.3%	19.6%	28.2%	25.0%	29.6%	45.5%	18.3%
Rhode Island	13.7%	13.6%	10.0%	25.0%	50.0%	0.0%	14.8%
South Carolina	13.3%	16.3%	31.4%	20.0%	30.7%	75.0%	18.5%
South Dakota	13.0%	20.0%	16.7%	50.0%	0.0%	0.0%	16.0%
Tennessee	16.4%	23.4%	30.0%	37.5%	26.8%	60.0%	20.5%
Texas	14.1%	23.5%	30.4%	44.4%	30.2%	27.3%	19.7%
Utah	10.8%	16.8%	25.0%	33.3%	25.8%	25.0%	15.5%
Vermont	12.5%	5.3%	9.1%	0.0%	10.0%	0.0%	10.3%
Virginia	12.7%	16.0%	23.0%	31.8%	22.4%	27.3%	15.8%
Washington	9.0%	14.1%	16.2%	16.7%	20.9%	11.1%	11.9%
West Virginia	15.8%	10.3%	25.9%	20.0%	15.8%	0.0%	16.6%
Wisconsin	9.5%	23.1%	25.0%	25.0%	37.7%	9.1%	16.5%
Wyoming	3.7%	11.1%	25.0%	0.0%	0.0%	0.0%	8.3%
Other	2.9%	0.0%	15.8%	50.0%	0.0%	0.0%	5.3%

Index of Tables

Index of Figures